Ce...
T...

Waris Dirie is an internationally renowned model and was a face of Revlon skin-care products. In 1997 she was appointed by the United Nations as special ambassador for women's rights in Africa, in its effort to eliminate the practice of female genital mutilation. In 2007 Waris Dirie was made a Chevalier de la Légion d'Honneur by the French Government.

Corinna Milborn is a political scientist and journalist in Austria, specialising in human rights issues. She is chief editor of the human rights magazine *Liga* and contributes to the news magazine *Format*.

Also by Waris Dirie

Desert Flower
Desert Dawn
Saving Safa

desert children

waris dirie

with corinna milborn

Translated by Sheelagh Alabaster

virago

VIRAGO

First published in Great Britain in 2005 by Virago Press
This edition published in 2007 by Virago Press

11 13 15 14 12 10

A CIP catalogue record for this book
is available from the British Library.

ISBN 978-1-84408-251-3

Typeset in New Baskerville by M Rules
Printed and bound in Great Britain by
Clays Ltd, St Ives plc

Papers used by Virago are from well-managed forests
and other responsible sources.

MIX
Paper from
responsible sources
FSC® C104740

Virago Press
An imprint of
Little, Brown Book Group
Carmelite House
50 Victoria Embankment
London EC4Y 0DZ

An Hachette UK Company
www.hachette.co.uk

www.virago.co.uk

Contents

Preface

Great Britain is a very special place for me. It was my first haven in Europe after my flight from Somalia and it is the country where I started my modelling career. It is also important to me because it has so many African things to offer.

British society is open to all sorts of cultures, traditions, languages and lifestyles. You can follow any religion, and nobody will bother you if you choose to wear your traditional clothes. This freedom and tolerance is one of Britain's greatest achievements. I think it makes the UK a colourful society and a model for other countries.

However, this tolerance can also mean that people outside an immigrant group are at times ignorant of its darker secrets. Tolerance can mislead people who might think it is OK – or even correct – to look away when somebody belonging to an ethnic minority is mistreated inside their own community, in the name of their traditions. Tolerance may mean that people feel uneasy about intervening or speaking out against traditional customs. This is especially cruel for those who have no say in their own communities; for some women and especially for many girls.

I have been fighting against the traditional practice of female circumcision – Female Genital Mutilation or FGM – for many years now, and although of course I knew there were women outside Africa, women in Europe, who were affected too, I was convinced that girls born in the UK – away from their villages, away from their grand-mothers – would be safe. But I was wrong.

The research for this book, which started in the UK, showed me that Female Genital Mutilation is a problem in Britain, and it is a problem that is hardly acknowledged. In London, Sheffield, Cardiff and many other cities in the UK, girls and women secretly suffer this unspeakably cruel tradition in the midst of an open, modern society. The British organization FORWARD, the Foundation for Women's Health, Research and Development, who cam-paign to see FGM recognised as a human rights violation and offer help and advice to women who are suffering from the effects of this practice, estimate that 80,000 women living in the UK have already been circumcised and live daily with the associated problems. And, alarm-ingly, 7000 girls now living in the UK are at high risk of being circumcised. These figures might well be modest, as we do not have exact figures for Arab and Asian women. Although FGM is seen largely as an African problem, it is also practised widely in Malaysia, Indonesia, Pakistan and

Iraq. We simply do not know the full extent of the number of women and girls who are affected.

Some of the women undergo the procedure, performed by midwives, doctors or even traditional cutter women, here in Europe. Many more go to the African or Arab countries their parents came from and have it done there. Virtually every girl from one of the communities who believe in this practice is at high risk. It is a fact that here, even in Britain in the twenty-first century, many of the mothers of girls in these groups remain convinced that their daughter will not find a husband if her genitals are intact. Men and women keep up the tradition, fired by a combination of fear and love. And because speaking out against FGM is still a taboo, nobody talks about it – it is kept secret. But inside the communities, everybody knows.

The UK was the first country in Europe to pass a law against female genital mutilation – in 1985 all forms of female circumcision were prohibited. And since 2003, the law has also prohibited parents or relatives taking their girls out of Britain to be circumcised back in their home countries. But, in all this time, not one person has been taken to court. Not one.

I believe it would not be difficult to stop this gruesome practice. I think what needs to happen first of all is for the laws and the reasons behind them to be made known to the people affected. They need to hear, in their own language, why FGM is bad – that it is both a cruel and a medically high-risk practice – and that it is illegal. Secondly, support for the women who are affected is desperately needed. Thirdly – and most contentiously – we need vigilance. I think doctors should examine girls when they are small, and check them again every year. Doctors, midwives and nurses check children for other health issues, and this is a health issue. Finally, the law must be enforced, and people suspected of being involved in carrying out this practice should be taken to court. France is the only country in Europe that has condemned parents and cutting women for practising FGM. But I assure you that the problem in the UK is no less serious.

I know that these demands are highly controversial among the African communities and also multicultural-ists. But there is just no gainsaying it: cutting a girl's genitals is one of the worst things you can do to a human being. We have to do everything possible to prevent it. I hope this book helps.

Waris Dirie 2005

desert children

I

my third life

I wake up bathed in sweat. It is very early still, not yet six o'clock. The night was short and troubled. I kept starting up out of heavy dark dreams. I close my eyes again but keep seeing the terrible images: a cheap hotel room, cramped and with yellowing wallpaper. There's a girl lying on the bed, maybe ten years old. She can't be more than twelve. She is naked. Four women are standing round the bed holding her down. The child's legs are spread open and an old woman sits in front of her with a scalpel in her hand. The sheet is soaked in blood. The girl lets out piercing screams. She keeps screaming. Her screams go right through my heart.

It was the screaming that kept waking me. It seems to be echoing round my own room. I stumble out of bed and get a glass of water. I look out of the window. It is starting to grow light. I am in Vienna and there is nobody screaming. It was only a dream, I tell myself.

It was only last night I got back from a weekend trip to Cardiff. Before I moved to Vienna I had spent a couple of years in the Welsh capital. I had really only wanted to catch up with some friends there and relax a bit and I had been looking forward to it, but that's not how it turned out. I was flying back that evening and friends had invited me over for lunch. We all knew each other from way back and there was a lot of talk and laughter: there was so much to say. But there was one young man – his name was Mariame –who was really quiet; he never said a word the whole time. He just kept looking over towards me, watching me intently during the meal. I had no idea why. When it was time for me to leave and I had said my goodbyes he walked me to the door, so I took the opportunity to ask what the matter was.

'Waris,' he told me. 'I really admire your strength. I never used to know that circumcision involved such agony for girls. I would like to help tell people about it. Most people just have no idea at all. The procedure just gets carried out because that's the way it's always been done. No one thinks about the consequences.'

I smiled. More and more men are coming over to the view that genital mutilation for girls is wrong. It gives me fresh hope. If only the whole thing were abolished and totally consigned to the past.

Suddenly Mariame turned very serious. 'But I wanted to tell you something else. A few days ago I heard this really awful story.' He went on to tell me about an African family in Cardiff that wanted to get their ten-year-old daughter circumcised. They took a hotel room and arranged for an old Libyan woman to be paid £200 for carrying out the cruel procedure there. But the knife slipped and the girl lost so much blood that she had to be taken to a doctor. 'And that's how I got to hear about it,' said Mariame. 'She nearly bled to death.'

'And didn't anyone tell the police?' I asked.

'I don't know,' he said.

'What's the family called? Where do they live? Is the girl alright now?' I kept on at him with my questions, but Mariame didn't know any of the details. 'That's why I feel so bad about it,' he said. 'I know that it happened but there's nothing I can do about it.'

It wasn't the first time I had heard about a genital mutilation case in Europe. The books I had written had made me a kind of symbolic figure in the campaign to abolish the practice of female circumcision, so people kept telling me about this ghastly ritual being carried out in Arab and African families. But whenever I tried to find out enough facts to be able to take the matter to the police, people would become evasive. It is well known in all the African communities that the practice won't stop at country borders, so there must be women and girls in Europe who are affected by it. Nobody would let on any more than that. There was only the one doctor or the one hospital here in Cardiff that was involved so I would be sure to be able to find something out.

I only had a short time left before my flight and I spent it talking to as many people as I could, phoning round all the Cardiff contacts I could think of. Had anyone heard anything? Did anyone have any idea who the girl was?

Nobody knew anything and, what is more, nobody was prepared even to talk about this kind of thing. I tried hospitals and the police and Social Services. Nothing. Time up. My flight back to Vienna was boarding. I left Cardiff behind, but inside I took with me the image of the girl in the hotel room. Deep inside – it invaded my dreams.

I can't get back to sleep; a waste of time trying. I find my trainers and put on my tracksuit to go for a run. Running is the best medicine for me, especially when I am really upset about something. Going for a jog will help to calm me down and it will clear my mind and let me think.

It's cold outside. Running along beside the river, I pass the first schoolchildren on their way. Gradually, my head clears. So good to be back in Austria, I think, relieved. The girls are safe here, no one will do that to them.

But how can I be so sure? What if the cases of genital mutilation that I've heard about here in Europe are not just exceptions? What if it is happening everywhere? Even here in Vienna? And I am back in my nightmare, hearing a girl screaming, somewhere in the middle of an industrial city in Europe.

I remember the interviews I gave when my books came out, the conferences I attended in my capacity as a special ambassador to the UN. It was always Africa we talked about and I always got asked about Somalia. Had I ever met an expert who knew about what was happening in Europe? No, that's not something I would have forgotten. I can't think of any research done on the subject or any statistics about genital mutilation in Europe. Are there more victims? I sit down on the nearest park-bench. Waris,

I tell myself, you've got to do something. You have to get the answers . . .

At that stage I was still hoping that my fears would prove groundless. Today I know that I was right in my assumptions about it happening all over. The decision to make this commitment to the campaign was to change my life. The time of Desert Flower and of Desert Dawn was over.

That was the morning my third life began.

All human beings are born free and equal in dignity and rights. They are endowed with reason and conscience and should act towards one another in a spirit of brotherhood. So says the Universal Declaration of Human Rights, the UN Resolution signed on 10 December 1948.

A week later I am sitting in a café on the Ringstrasse in Vienna. Red and white trams rattle past the window. The buildings over the road are old and quite grand. Around me people are sitting at tables reading newspapers. Some stay for hours, only ordering one cup of coffee, but nobody minds. Typical of Vienna: it is really easygoing here, and I love the atmosphere. I have been here a year now and I really like it. I am often asked, why Vienna? And I always say the same thing: Vienna is a beautiful city. I have made a lot of new friends here. Yes, and I feel I am at home, I have finally arrived.

There's been a lot of travelling in the last few years. As a UN special ambassador I was giving lectures all over the world and I was making a lot of charity function appearances, but I always felt I wasn't doing enough. I decided to take a lead: here in Vienna I started up the Waris Dirie Foundation. We have a small team collecting donations for projects in my native Somalia campaigning for an end to the practice of genital mutilation.

At the present time Somalia is a long way away for me. I am waiting for Corinna. She is a political science writer and a journalist. We have often worked together. Mostly she will do research for me, collecting data about women in Africa and the projects on the go over there highlighting the need to stop female genital mutilation. A few days ago I asked her to drop everything else and get me as much information as she possibly could about the situation for women in Europe. She arrives a bit late but I'm easy with that, having a very relaxed attitude to time-keeping and appointments myself. I'm really keen to see what she has managed to get for me.

Corinna sits down, plonking a huge green box file on the table. She's breathless: 'There's everything I've found out in there.' She orders a coffee and starts to open up the file. It has hundreds and hundreds of pages. Taking one of the pages in her hand she leans over towards me and whispers, 'You're right. Everyone likes to think that female genital mutilation is on the wane, but that's not what's happening at all. It's being practised in more and more countries in Asia – and Europe as well – but there's hardly any information about it.'

So it's true. In Arab countries, in the Yemen, in Pakistan, I had learned of thousands of girls having their genitals removed. More and more cases were coming to light in Indonesia and Malaysia. And now in Europe as well. I had only known a fraction of what was going on there and assumed it was of marginal significance. That was what I had thought until now.

Corinna closes the file up and pushes it over to me. 'It's best if you look through my notes yourself. You'll see straightaway how big the problem already is here in Europe.'

I open the file and look at the first page, skim the text with the masses of margin notes Corinna has scribbled. Something catches my eye. There is a list of the names of women who have suffered the greatest injustice that can be inflicted on our sex: FGM, female genital mutilation, or MSF, *mutilations sexuelles feminines,* female circumcision, the Arabic word 'khafd'. *Be careful!* says Corinna's pencilled note. *Many of the victims object to the use of the term 'circumcision' because it seems to play down the extent of the damage done.*

'That's right,' I tell Corinna. 'Circumcision sounds like male circumcision but it's nothing like it at all. Although I honestly don't mind what term people use, I just want it to stop. FGM is pure violence against women, a breach of human rights. The United Nations has said so.' Corinna nods and leafs through her pile of papers, pulling out a copy of the UN Declaration of 1993. United Nations and World Health Organisation estimates put the figures for female circumcision victims at a hundred and fifty million. A hundred and fifty million women and girls! In all probability the actual numbers will be far higher. Many countries are considered blind spots where it is impossible to get any data, and nobody knows how many victims are involved in those places. A hundred and fifty million women and girls – that is more people than there are in the whole of Germany, Switzerland, Austria, the Netherlands, Belgium and Denmark put together. Victims include week-old babies, girls at puberty and grown women of thirty.

Every time I talk about female genital mutilation I think of what happened to me. I am five years old again and I am sitting on a rock back at home in Somalia. It is early in the morning. I am afraid. I'm sitting sort of in my mother's lap – her legs are encircling me – and she puts a bit of broken-off root in my mouth to stop me biting off my tongue with the pain. 'Waris,' she says, 'you know I won't be able to hold you still. I'm on my own here with you. So be good, my little one. Be brave, for my sake, then it'll soon be over.'

I can see again the harsh, ugly face of the old woman and the fierce looks she gives me with her dead-seeming eyes. I can see the old carpet bag, see her taking out the rusty razor blade in her long fingers, can see the dried blood on the blade. My mother blindfolds me. Then I feel my own flesh being cut, my genitals being sliced away. I have never been able to describe what this felt like. There are no words which can give the measure of the pain. I can hear the sound of the blunt blade hacking away again and again at my skin. I remember how my legs were shaking, I remember all the blood and I remember trying so hard to sit still. I hear myself calling out prayers to heaven. Finally, I fall into a faint. When I come round my first thought is that it's over now, at least. The blindfold has slipped off. I can see her clearly, the old butcher-woman, and I can see the pile of acacia thorns at her side. When she starts to push them through my flesh the pain is excruciating. She threads white cotton through the puncture holes she has made, sewing me up.

My legs go dead. The pain is driving me mad. I have only one thought in my mind: I want to die.

I see my mother's face now as if it were yesterday. She is utterly convinced that she is doing the right thing for me. The only thing that is right. I don't know how many times I have told this story now. Each time it seems like it happened to somebody else, some other little girl. As if that little Waris was someone else.

'Can I get you anything else to drink?' asks the waiter; he is friendly and polite, and dressed in the usual formal black and white. I am quite startled and look at him blankly, then quickly order an orange juice. I wonder if he has any idea what vale of shadows I have just been walking through . . . Corinna is deep in her pile of papers. Or she is pretending to be. At any rate, she is sensitive enough to know not to ask me what the trouble is. A little girl at the next table looks at me and catches my eye, laughing.

I quickly take out another research paper. It is about the medical effects of circumcision. I won't have to read it, I know all about them already: pain on menstruating, the dangers of infection, the fear of anyone touching you. An old saying from Somalia comes back to me: 'Love hurts three times – when they cut you, when you are married and when you give birth.' Women who have been mutilated and infibulated are cut open a little way after the marriage ceremony and when the baby is due. 'Perhaps the worst thing for us women, though, is the one that isn't here at all,' I tell Corinna. 'It's the terrible, unwritten law that demands your silence. You must never tell anyone about the pain.'

I have to pause. I take another sip of juice. Much of

what I am reading here I have experienced myself. I know these pains, but time is kind to my memory and at least not all the experiences are still constantly at the forefront of my mind. But they are on instant recall, as if they had never gone away.

'Did you find anything, any data about FGM in Europe?' I ask Corinna. She fishes a piece of paper out of the pile and shows me the statistics she has scribbled down. *France 70,000*, it says. *Great Britain 80,000. Italy 35,000*. What? What do these numbers mean? There is a list of some African and some Arab states, and then some percentages. Underneath, there it is, underlined twice and written in red felt tip: *500,000*. I shake my head in disbelief. 'What's this number? 500,000 whats? Not women who've been mutilated? Living in Europe? It can't be true.'

Corinna nods, but before she can speak I interrupt. 'Wait,' I say, in shock. I can't believe we're talking about half a million women in Europe who have suffered FGM. 'Where does this figure come from? What evidence have you got?'

According to Corinna there are many European countries that have exact statistics about women immigrants coming from countries where FGM is practised. The World Health Organisation has data about the percentage of women in those countries who are mutilated in this way. That's how the number of affected women is calculated. 'But we haven't got figures for all of the countries, of course,' says Corinna. 'And lots of African and Arab and Asian women just don't have any papers, so they don't appear in the statistics.'

I look at her, a question in my eyes. She swallows before she speaks: 'That means our half a million is only the starting point.'

I have to take a deep breath. My vision starts to blur, my head swims. Half a million girls and women in Europe have gone through this: five hundred thousand with daughters of their own, who will be insisting on the ritual all the more when they see they are not accepted into Western society. Half a million victims here at our front door, and probably more arriving every day. And nobody knows about it. Nobody does anything about it. I want to know more about this. Who are these women? What are their conditions like, here in Europe? Are there laws and regulations to help them, people they can turn to? How are their daughters treated and is anyone working on this anywhere in Europe?

Again I think of the young girl in that hotel room in Cardiff. A girl who will never recover from the physical and emotional damage done to her that day. 'Five hundred thousand women means five hundred thousand potential mothers. We have to reach these women, reach out to them and help them.'

I close the box-file and make my decision. From now on I am going to give myself over to a campaign to fight female genital mutilation in Europe. I will go on until every child here is safe. Until everyone is quite clear: FGM is not a question of culture. FGM is a question of torture.

I was not to know at that time what a long and difficult journey I was setting out on.

As I say goodbye to Corinna she tells me, 'Take a look on the Internet at the discussion websites on the subject.

People can contribute on message boards – it's anonymous, so they can write whatever they like. You'll be
surprised how many people will talk openly about FGM in
a forum like that.'

   'Corinna, you know I don't have a computer at home.
I don't know much about using the internet, but of
course I want to know about it. Why don't we meet up
tomorrow in the office? You can help me and direct me to
the right websites,' I tell her.

The next day we are sitting at the office computer at the
Waris Dirie Foundation. Out of the window there is a
wonderful view of Vienna. I can see the Danube and the
mountains beyond, so peaceful and harmonious. It is in
stark contrast to the world I am about to enter.

   Corinna types in the first internet address. A page
comes up with a purple header. Several contributions to
the forum are displayed and I click on the first article. A
jolt goes through me. Here is a woman who has undergone genital mutilation herself; she is detailing what
unbearable agony she had to endure when her child was
born because the vagina was not able to stretch to accom-
modate the child. 'I nearly died,' she writes.

   I am absolutely riveted and cannot take my eyes off
the text. I have hardly ever heard anyone speak as directly
as this about FGM. I click again – and keep clicking.

   Medyna: I was mutilated when I was twelve years old
   and now I am nineteen. I can remember it as if it
   were yesterday. Since it happened I have lost the
   will to go on. I've tried to kill myself several times

and I can't bear it if a man tries to touch me. I've vowed never to have sexual relationships because I would be so ashamed. Please help me – it's not easy to talk about it; this is the first time I've ever told anyone.

Mya: I'm from Mali. I have French citizenship. I was taken to Mali when I was thirteen and that's when they cut me.

Marissam: When I slept with my boyfriend I couldn't feel anything – no pleasure. But because I know that he likes it when I say, 'oh, that's good, keep doing that', well, I would just say it, so that at least one of us was getting something out of it. It is really hard to not feel a thing when you make love to someone you love. Very, very hard!!!

Samia: I was very young when I was circumcised. I don't remember it. I suffered a lot because I didn't understand. As a young woman I had relationships but I never felt any pleasure.

Maia: I don't really know anything about Genital Mutilation. I went through it when I was very small. I can't remember anything about it. One day my mother told me about it. People told me I wouldn't enjoy sleeping with a boy. I was frightened. I had problems with men because I wouldn't go to bed with them. I thought it wouldn't work with me. I cannot understand why anyone supports the idea of genital mutilation. People like that make me so angry. I didn't ask to have it done. Who has the right to take away something that belongs to me?

The desert children – here they speak openly. In the anonymity of the web they are not afraid to tell their stories. Here they can swap experiences with fellow victims, get advice – here for many of them there is a chance to express their pain. For an hour I kept on reading the different accounts, dozens of them. Some of them really touched me, from girls who have no one else to talk to apart from on the web with its anonymous safety. Why won't anyone speak about the nightmare anywhere else?

These women are in urgent need of support. Problems like these cannot be solved when you are on your own. I read some more contributions, and come across 'Kadi'. She seems to spend a lot of time in the chat-rooms, sometimes she writes something every day. I open up one of her messages at random and I can't stop reading:

> Please help me! I was circumcised when I was four years old. To get it done my parents took me back to our own country. I don't want to have a relationship at all. Can you tell me, if you have undergone the same procedure as me, tell me what you feel? Is it true what the doctors say?
>
> Thank you, all of you, anyone who will help me. I feel so desperate.

There's something about her that troubles me. Perhaps it is her straightforward way of writing or the insecurity she displays in coming to terms with her own body, with her sexuality. At any rate, the driving force in her life reminds me very much of my own. That's why I suddenly decide to contact her. *Dear Kadi,* I write, *I have read your contributions to the forum and am very affected by what you say. You have to realise that you are not on your own with your problems. If I can help you in any way, write to me.*

Then I have had enough and shut down the computer.

A few days later Kadi writes back. We are in frequent contact from then on. She describes her life and I tell her about the plans I have to take up the fight against FGM in Europe.

'I was born twenty years ago in Paris and I live with my sister in the 14th arrondissement,' she writes. 'My parents are from Mali, from the region known as Ethnie Bambara. My father's marriage is polygamous; he had three wives and twenty-two children in all. My mother died six years ago as a result of a doctor's mistake made when I was born. I only found out about it recently and it shook me to the core. I am convinced she wouldn't have died if she hadn't had the genital mutilation.

'I respect the fact that my father is polygamous. Having three mothers was never anything difficult for me to accept. Nearly all families in Mali are polygamous. My cousin is twenty-seven and she's been living in France for two years. Her husband only has the one wife and she's always complaining about it – I can't understand her. She says, when she dies he will have nobody to look after him . . .

'My father has thirteen daughters. Eleven of them he has had circumcised. The two eldest were born in Mali so

he didn't have any trouble getting it done. The third was
born in France and was mutilated here before the 1983
regulation outlawing the practice. Where it was done and
who carried it out I don't know.

'When it came to my turn it was done on a trip back to
Mali with my mother, in a bush, far away from my father's
village. I remember they hurt me a lot. But I only had
vague memories and wasn't sure what had been done
until I saw pictures of another case and I read the text.
Then I understood. It shocked me.

'I must have been five years old. My cousin told me
later on that I had nearly died. I remember bleeding and
bleeding and the blood not stopping. When we got back
to France the woman who had done the circumcision lost
her job because nobody would entrust their daughter to
her anymore. She had a finger missing.

'I remember the grown-ups holding me down, hanging
on to my arms and legs. I remember I was lashing out with
all my might and that I was yelling really loud. Then I
remember they tied a strange bit of cloth round my waist,
to be pants of sorts, and I remember the white flesh showing between my legs. I know I was in shock and couldn't
walk. I cried and cried until I had no more tears. (. . .)
When I think of what they did to me as a young girl, and
with no anaesthetic, it makes me shudder.

'After that I kept getting nightmares. I was scared they
would attack my two little sisters because they had not
been touched yet. Not a day goes by without my thinking
of what happened. When I see my friends from school or
just some women in the street or on the underground, I
think about the fact that they haven't had anything taken

away, so why did it have to happen to me? Perhaps it's just life. *C'est la vie.*

'I've even thought of going to a psychologist to get help because I've got no one else to talk to – nobody in my family and nobody else I know. (. . .) FGM as a topic is totally taboo. My father never mentioned it to us and I never heard him speak of it to anyone else. One of my stepmothers is for it and the other is against it. The second one has even managed to talk her own younger sister out of having her other daughter done in spite of threats from the police who had caught wind of the disaster caused to her first child. (. . .)

'I feel handicapped today. In your book "Desert Flower" I recognised myself, Waris. I was afraid of boys for a long time and had vowed never to have sex. I have only ever had one boyfriend. I'm still with him. We've been together for a year and three months but nothing happens between us. I've told him I prefer to wait until I'm married, and I say it's because of my religion, I'm a Muslim. But that's not the real reason. His family are from Mali as well but he has no idea about it and I don't know how to tell him. I really don't want to tell him at all but one day I'll have to tell a man. I don't need to at the moment.

'It's true that men, especially those who were born in France, have no idea what happens to their sisters back home. I don't think my brothers have the slightest inkling. Nobody talks about it at home. I've never told anyone what I've just told you. It is good to be able to tell someone.'

In the past few months I've read and re-read Kadi's e-mails. They gave me the strength to go on when work was getting on top of me. Kadi came to be my guiding light, my beacon. The fate she had suffered served as a warning and as a challenge at the same time. I understood from her that circumcised women in Europe suffer from a further problem, namely having to live in two separate worlds: the African world of their parents and the European world they were born into and in which they grew up.

In my home country it is, regrettably, the norm to be mutilated. The women do not know it any other way and they all have problems with it – but they are all having to cope with the same problems. But the young women that grow up in Europe have to contend with knowing they are different. It is a heavy burden: they can't tell a soul without bringing shame on their family and on their culture. I have given lectures in a number of schools in Europe. The pupils, girls as well as boys, are always horrified. What causes this strong reaction amongst young people who come from the same cultures? How must they be feeling when the talk is of 'barbaric practices' and 'indescribable torture'? It's their own families we're discussing. No wonder that most of them clam up and prefer to keep their problems to themselves.

I have got a group of friends together to do some research: Corinna is with us and then there's Lea and Julia, two young journalists. They all know a great deal about human rights questions. We are all convinced that genital mutilation is a major issue here in Europe. There are thousands of victims in every country in Europe – and there are thousands of people who know who carries out these procedures and where it is done. But apart from this inner circle of women in the know, nobody else gets to hear about it. The net seems to be pretty tight. I can't believe it.

We are meeting in a tiny fish restaurant in the food market. This is one of my favourite spots in Vienna, the Naschmarkt: mountains of fruit and vegetables on sale, traders from all over the world. With all its colour and the comings and goings it reminds me of markets back home in Somalia. You can even get exotic African specialities like manioc and plantain. Julia and Corinna are already there when I arrive; they are sitting at a table, deep in discussion, with a pile of files and folders in front of them. I take over – 'Food first!' – and push all the paperwork to one side.

At last Lea turns up. She has concentrated on Austria in her research. This is a country where the legislation is less vague on FGM than in many other European states. There has been a special clause in the penal code about it since 2002. FGM is treated as actual bodily harm and carries a penalty of up to ten years' imprisonment. The fact that we have this legislation is due to some undercover research carried out by the Austrian news magazine *profil* in 2001, trying to find out whether there were any doctors in Austria prepared to carry out genital mutilation. 'I followed up the story and got to speak to some of the people involved,' Lea says. We were shocked by what she went on to tell us.

Ala (the name has been changed) was born in Austria. Her father is Arabian, her mother Austrian. She went to a doctor and told him she was Arabian and was planning to

marry an Egyptian man. Her problem was that she was
not a virgin and she wanted to undergo at her fiancé's
wish a 'purifying circumcision'. The doctor agreed at
once to perform the operation. He would bring the necessary instruments and medication. He had bought some
of the equipment from a hospital in Vienna and some of
it from a flea market. 'Don't worry,' he said. 'It's not rusty
old knives.'

He suggested doing the operation in a private apartment because this would enable the patient to rest
properly after the procedure. There was always the
danger of heavy bleeding. He said that he did not, himself, have a surgery, but that he could borrow rooms from
a colleague at a surgery for seventy euros any time he
needed to, or he could use the rooms of a female colleague he had already consulted about it. He would like
to video the operation. 'Then I can drive you home afterwards. In a situation like that it would be much better
than taking the tram,' he offered. After a number of pre-
liminary consultations an appointment was made for the
operation. The procedure would be carried out in two
stages. It was at this point that Ala called it off. The doctor
phoned her at least twenty times in the weeks that followed. He wanted to carry out the operation at all costs.
He even offered to do it for free, as a 'wedding present'
and he would only charge the seventy euros for the room
rent.

The team from the magazine *profil* contacted the surgeon a few weeks later and confronted him with the
results of their undercover research. His lame excuse was
that he was only going to carry out the procedure if it

were all legal and above board. And of course, he wanted to prevent further risk. 'If Ala had gone to someone else there would have been the danger she might have lost the entire clitoris. That would have been a surgical disaster,' he said.

'I did some research', says Lea, indignant about what she has found out. 'That doctor is still in practice. But at least that case led to the law being changed. Now in Austria it is illegal to carry out genital mutilation even when the woman in question requests the procedure herself.'

'Well, that's a start. That doesn't sound bad at all.'

'Yes, on paper it looks good,' Lea continues. 'But the reality is a different matter. So far not a single case has gone to trial. Not a single victim has testified, not a single doctor has been charged.'

'That's unbelievable,' I say.

'No, really. I'll give you another example. Parents who wanted to have their daughter circumcised in Africa are seen by the law to be inciting a crime. But nobody has ever been charged. In spite of the fact that lots of people know that girls are circumcised when they go back home for holidays and that it happens here, too.'

'But why are no charges brought?' I ask. 'There must be organisations that are in the know!'

'Because it's like that in all other European countries,' Lea answers. 'I think it's because these organisations are scared they would lose the relationship they have with the African community if they started getting charges brought. Because if you talk, you're a traitor.'

I shake my head in disbelief, and pull out a report by

the African Women's Organisation, a group based here in Vienna. Lea has summarised the most important results from a survey conducted with African immigrants in Austria. It shocks me: 30.5 percent of those interviewed get their daughters circumcised. More than three quarters do it because 'it's a question of tradition', nearly half of them think FGM is 'good for the morals of a woman' and a quarter say that the procedure gives women 'more control over their sexuality'. Most of the people surveyed who will get their daughters circumcised say they go back to Africa to have it done – but the operations carried out in Europe account for 11.5 percent. Of these again, 1.9 percent are done in Austria, and 9.6 percent in Germany or Holland.

I go over the figures again and do some calculations: 'That means thousands of genital mutilation procedures have taken place in Europe,' I exclaim in surprise. Can that really be the case? Can it be that thousands of girls have been subject to this cruel torture right here under our noses – and nobody noticed? Where are the people who are doing this? Is it doctors doing it? Nurses? Medical amateurs?

Soon afterwards I was to find out that the answers to my questions were to be found right outside my front door.

According to the report by the African Women's Organisation, there are 8000 mutilated women living in Austria alone. How do people treat them here, in a country where hardly anyone has even heard of FGM? What happens when they get to know a man or when they have to go to a doctor for anything? And, vitally, how do we get them to realise they must stop putting their own daughters through the same awful experience? Gradually I come to see that it is not merely a question of finding out who the people are who are carrying out the operations in Europe: it is equally important to support the women who have already been subjected to the process before they arrived here in Europe. Where I come from it is sadly seen as 'normal' to have been circumcised. But here? People are horrified at the very mention of it and they turn away in disgust. This I know from experience.

For me the worst thing is that, wherever I go, everyone knows what happened to me. I am not seen first and foremost as a woman, because they think of me as the 'woman who's been circumcised'. When I was writing my first book I bared my soul, announcing in public, 'Look what happened to me. They took my genitals and cut them, mutilating me in the cruellest way.' Since then, whenever I meet someone all they really want to ask me is what I look like down there and if I can have sex and how. They don't have to say anything; I can feel it in the way they look at me. Perhaps it is worse when they don't mention it at all but just stare at me.

I know most of them mean well. Many of them want to help me and they want to be supportive. Often the good intentions turn out not to be such a good thing in the end.

Here is an example. A year ago there was a fair on in Austria and my books were on display at one of the stalls. Donations for my Somalia projects were being collected.

When I arrived, the first thing I saw was a huge yellow
poster with a photo of a circumcision operation taking
place. I was even more shocked to read the text on the
poster, which said in big letters *Come and meet circumcision
victim Waris Dirie.* What gives them the right to treat me
like that? Just imagine a woman asking for donations to a
fund for abused children and posters saying *Come and
meet the victim of childhood abuse, Stella Stereotype.** Would
you even dream of asking her right at the start of every
interview what it was like when she was abused as a seven-
year-old by her uncle? Of course not. It is vital to respect
people's privacy.

As victims of FGM we are not shown such sensitivity.
People point at us, calling the societies we come from
barbaric and backward, but at the same time they seem
unaware just how barbarically we are treated here in
Europe. This all comes back to me when I am talking to
Ishraga Hamid. We meet in her flat in Vienna, where she
greets me and invites me to sit down in the living room.
She's wearing a brightly-coloured African dress.

Ishraga's full name is Ishraga Hamid Mustafa, she has
a master's degree in media studies and journalism and
she is from the Sudan. She is forty-three now and went to
university in Khartoum and then later in Austria and she
works as a Reader in the Institute of Political Sciences at
Vienna University. Between 1997 and 2004 she carried
out a number of research projects about the conditions of
various groups of women in Vienna: black, African,

*Translator's note: My invented English equivalent of the origi-
nal German, 'Marta Mustermann'.

Muslim, Arabian. She knows what it is like to live as an African woman in Europe.

I am struck by how pleasantly softly spoken this slight figure of a woman is. She is open and friendly and her voice is that of a young girl. However gentle her manner may be, she comes over as confident and determined. The results of her research leave little room for doubt or illusions. Only three percent of the African women interviewed have jobs commensurate with their qualifications, although eighty percent of them have had full school education and thirty-seven percent are graduates. 'I had to go to work as a cleaner, to start with, myself,' says Ishraga Hamid.

'That certainly won't be helping women to feel at home here,' I put in.

She nods. 'Eighty percent of women say they don't feel at home in Vienna and all of them say they are discriminated against on grounds of their skin colour, their origins or their sex Europeans often have a stereotypical view of African women that is sexist and racist. A typical response from an Austrian man in a survey conducted in 2001 puts it succinctly: "European women are good in the office and African women are good in bed."'

Another of Ishraga Hamid's projects deals with the topic of Reproductive Health and it also treats the issue of circumcision. 'I have always refused to look at this cruel ritual out of context. Female genital mutilation will only be abolished if women's socio-political situation as a whole is taken into account.'

'What about men's role?' I ask. 'I think it is a key factor.'

'Many men are against the practice back home in the countries we come from, but there are no scientific studies about what the majority of men really think on this matter. All the research so far concentrates on us women. An astonishing thing is that many of the women surveyed actually support the concept of circumcision.'

'I know – even though I don't understand it. Genital mutilation causes such pain. All of us as women know that.'

'In my view, women support the practice not because they want it but because they are financially totally dependent on their men. They use sexuality to keep their menfolk satisfied.'

'Do you think a change in the law will help to get rid of FGM?'

'On their own laws won't do it, but they are a first step. There has been a law in the Sudan for ages that forbids the practice of female circumcision, but it has had no effect at all. What we need to campaign for is education, and it must be women themselves who carry the message. What women need to be educated about covers more than just circumcision; they need to realise what rights they have – the right to determine the size of their families and to have a say in when they want children, if they want them at all.'

'There are some anti-FGM groups already running education programmes on those lines,' I say.

'But they should be taking the other topics on board as well.'

At first I am disappointed. I really had wanted to work intensively with the anti-FGM pressure groups in the various countries, and to find out as much as possible about them. Now it is becoming clear that these groups have hardly any money for this education work. They are not strong enough as organisations to have a real voice. And they are operating in a kind of grey area.

When I leave Ishraga Hamid's flat, it has turned cold. Autumn is on its way. I snuggle down inside my jacket. Waris, I tell myself, it's time to roll up your sleeves and get down to it. You will have to do something yourself.

You don't often see black women in the streets in Austria. After speaking to Ishraga Hamid I know that most of them are not happy here, although their lives in Africa were very hard. In my own country of Somalia women are still often regarded as their husband's 'property' because they can be bought and sold like cattle. But it is the women who bear the burden of all the everyday tasks. It is the women who give birth to the children and it is the women who feed the family. At the same time, they have no rights whatsoever: they cannot hold property or be entitled to a pension or social security provision. In the frequent outbreaks of civil war, they, like the children, are among the first victims. It is the case in the Sudan, in Somalia, in Congo, in Tanzania. Even in peacetime there is a hidden war, a war against women: they are beaten and oppressed. And mutilated.

But African women are not weak. On the contrary, there are many who stand up for themselves and fight for their rights. Things *are* changing. In some African countries, the fossilised social structures are beginning to waver, but fundamental change will take time. So for

many victims the only way out is to run away. Not many
women will manage to escape. Some of them land up in
Austria, one of the world's richest countries. The money
you spend in a restaurant here would be enough to keep
a whole African family for a week, or even for a month.

'Women who run away from home to escape FGM
won't have problems getting asylum in Austria, will they?'
I ask Lea.

'You'd be surprised,' she replies. 'Austria still does not
officially recognise FGM as grounds for granting asylum.
When I asked one of the officials why this was he told
me – unofficially of course – that it is difficult to know if
the women are telling the truth.'

There have been fewer than ten instances of asylum
granted on the grounds of FGM. The first time was on 21
May 2002, to a woman from Cameroon. She had been
promised, without her knowledge, to an old man there. As
she was not a virgin, she was supposed to undergo infibulation, one of the most serious forms of genital mutilation,
before the marriage took place. I wanted to know how
authorities in Europe dealt with women who sought their
help. I contacted Joy (not her real name), an asylum
seeker from Nigeria. She lives in a refugee hostel in a
European city but I am not going to say which city. The
family pursuing the young woman has a very long arm.

Joy is striking is appearance. She is tall, her make-up is
perfect and her hair is smooth and blow-dried into style.
She is from an educated family, high up in society, has
been to university in the States and speaks excellent
English. The other residents of the refugee hostel do not
know her problems. Likewise, she knows nothing of

theirs. People don't talk about it, she tells me on the way over to the hostel. They are all here for very different reasons and they come from a wide range of cultural backgrounds. The women in the hostel are forced to put up with things together.

We go up to the first floor, meeting a few of the other women in the corridor and on the stairs. I am struck by their poverty and their despair. In these desolate surroundings it is a relief to hear the happy voices of some children. Joy checks in quickly with the social worker on duty, because there are strict rules here about visiting. Visitors may only be seen in a special room and they have to sign in and out. The visitors' room is dilapidated and cramped, with a small table in the corner, and a couple of plastic chairs and a worn-out couch as the only seating. There are no pictures or posters to brighten the yellowing bare walls.

We sit at the table and Joy tells me her story, gesticulating as she speaks. She keeps stopping, rolling her eyes in frustration, or hitting the table with the flat of her hand to show her anger. She is neither allowed to work nor to move around as she chooses, she complains. When her daughter wants anything new, usually something that the other children at school have all got, Joy has to explain that she can't have it. She hates to do this but she only has the three hundred euros allowance for the whole month and she needs all that for food. This strong and resolute woman has been waiting for more than eighteen months for a decision on her asylum application. She's been turned down once already but has gone to appeal. It is getting her down, you can see.

'Why did you come here as a refugee?' I ask her. Her
story is a long one. And sad. Joy is from a part of Nigeria
where genital mutilation is not practised. But when she
met and fell in love with a man from a different ethnic
background she went to live with him in another part of
the country. Only then did she realise that women there
were cut. Joy's husband had never mentioned it. He was
not bothered by the fact that she was not circumcised.

The difficulties began when Joy became pregnant.
Right from the start she was afraid the baby would be a
girl and that she would be forced by her husband and
his family to have the child circumcised. She was really
against the idea and got very upset. At last she told her
husband how worried she was and he reacted very sym-
pathetically. He told her she was the mother of the child
and therefore would be the one to look after the baby.
He even swore on the Koran that he would not permit
circumcision of the child. But it turned out differently.
When the baby arrived it was a girl. Her husband's
family insisted that the young couple move in with them.
They said it would be so difficult for the couple to bring
up a child on their own, and the money side of things
would be a problem otherwise, too. Extended families
are the norm in Nigeria. Joy's husband's family was
huge – about forty people altogether, what with all the
unmarried sisters, the brothers and their wives, and the
nephews.

For Joy a hard time was about to begin. The family
started to go on about having the baby circumcised. All
three of Joy's sisters-in-law told her she must have her
daughter circumcised and cited a variety of reasons: to

make her a good wife, to make sure she would not become a prostitute, to make sure she was not dirty . . . In this culture it was held to be a gross insult to tell someone, 'Your wife is uncircumcised!' Joy went to her husband, but he just said the women should sort it out amongst themselves.

She takes a deep breath and continues. At first her sisters-in-law had wanted to have the baby done at the age of forty days but Joy had been unwell, so they waited. They began going on about it again when the little one was nearly two years old. They were quite open in discussing this normally taboo topic – a shock to Joy, on whom they were putting pressure.

Joy went to a doctor for help and he advised her to keep coming up with excuses. So she said the child was running a fever. And then there was something different. In this way she was able to put it off, time and again. However, when the child was two and a half the pressure became such that she decided to run away. Not because she hated her husband, but he was too weak to stand up against the wishes of his family. Joy was forced to make the choice between him and her child: she decided to save her daughter.

Getting to Europe was quite an ordeal. It took all her savings to pay for her ticket. In order to save her daughter the torture of genital mutilation Joy would have to go through so much more. When she had been living with her husband's family she had heard so many awful things. There had been the circumcised two-year-old who cried every time she had to go to the toilet until, in the end, they had to take her to hospital and get her opened up again; and the girl who had been sewn up and got an infection that had to be treated in hospital.

Joy lowers her voice and tells me what horrifies her most: it is the way the procedures are carried out on children. The women performing the mutilation – usually old women – cut the little girls without using any anaesthetic. It is agonising to the children, and the sound of their screams is unbearable.

I take a deep breath. I know only too well what the procedure is like. 'What was it like arriving here in Europe? How were you treated?' I ask her.

When she arrived in the country, Joy lodged an application for asylum. She explained to the official that she had fled her home country in order to save her daughter from forced genital mutilation. The authorities turned down her application and wanted to deport her to Britain because that had been the country she had reached first, even though she had travelled straight on from there and did not stay in England – her brother-in-law lives in England and is still insisting the girl must be circumcised, and if necessary the procedure would be done at his home. Joy looks in her handbag and fishes out a piece of paper. It is an e-mail her sister-in-law had sent her. Joy has no idea how her sister-in-law found out her e-mail address. The arm of the family is indeed long.

She passes me the e-mail and I read it straightaway. The message is very clear: unless the daughter is circumcised she cannot become a proper Muslim and she cannot expect to have a happy life. They insist the operation is carried out. They say it is a ritual that is important to any family.

Being part of a tightly-knit extended family can be a wonderful thing. I have a large family myself and my relatives are all over the world, with a brother in Holland, my sister in Switzerland and an aunt in the States. Although we are far apart we all stay in contact and if one of us needs help the rest of the family bands together in support. But each respects the lifestyle of the other members of the family and nobody tells the others what to do or how to behave. This support network is marvellous, but for Joy the net was more like a trap.

I read the e-mail again. Joy will only be safe where the family has no access to her daughter. If she is deported to Britain or back to Africa, her daughter will be in danger. Why on earth can't the authorities see that? Why is there no room on this rich continent for one woman and her small daughter?

What is life like generally for women asylum seekers in European countries? I phone Corinna and ask her and the others to pull this information together for me. We meet up again in the office a few days later.

'It's not good news.' This is how Corinna starts the discussion. 'It is the same situation all over Europe – just like it is in Austria. FGM is not recognised anywhere as automatically giving grounds for asylum.'

'But why not? Genital mutilation can't be counted as less important than suffering torture!' I object. You have a right to political asylum in Europe if you are subjected to torture and are able to provide credible evidence. Yet if a woman is tortured because in her homeland a woman does not count, that is obviously not enough.

Lea reports back about the situation in Germany and tells us, 'The law in Germany seems to be pretty vague and chaotic on this subject. Although there *is* a law there that states that persecution of women is also grounds for granting asylum, when it comes down to it it seems to be a lottery.'

She passes me a few pages of notes she has written. It says that in 2002, in Aachen, a thirty-six-year-old Nigerian woman and her three-year-old daughter were granted asylum as victims of political persecution. The court had argued that in Nigeria there was a high risk of women and girls being subjected to genital mutilation because the state does not provide sufficient protection. It goes on to say that a woman asylum seeker from Guinea had her application granted in Berlin in 2003, with the judges arguing as follows:

The practice is considered the norm in all strata of society, in all the regions and among all the ethnic groups. It is particularly of note that a woman has little chance of being accepted in marriage unless circumcision has been performed. There is thus no chance for a woman to move to a safer part of the country. (. . .) Female circumcision is a procedure which is no less intense in effect than any torture.

This is good to read. 'Here we have it in black and white at last,' I say to Corinna and Lea. 'Mutilation is just as bad as torture. It *is* torture.'

But not all the German courts are deciding like that, as Lea had already hinted. I go on reading: On 2 December

2003 a court in Freiburg im Breisgau turns down an application from a woman from Guinea. The same thing
happens to a woman from Togo at a court in Oldenburg.
The opinion of the court states that the woman's age pre-
cludes the threat of genital mutilation. How is a German
court going to know that? I am relieved to read that at
least the woman was not deported and that she went on to
win on appeal. Then we have a woman from Sierra Leone
whose application is turned down by a court in Frankfurt
on the grounds that 'this is not a case of political persecution, as FGM is seen as an initiation rite with the
express purpose of admitting a girl as a full member of
the community. Thus it cannot be said that persecution is
taking place with the purpose of excluding an individual.'

'What cynical rubbish,' I exclaim. 'That's appalling.
These women are completely at the mercy of the whims of
these judges in Germany.'

'It is no better in Britain,' explains Corinna. 'In many
cases women have been deported. Jeff Rooker, Minister of
State for the Home Office, told Parliament in 2001 that
this kind of threat did not come under the convention
about the treatment of refugees unless the government of
the applicant's country of origin officially supports FGM.'

'I don't care if the government of a country supports
the practice or not,' I object, 'if women are at risk. And
the figures prove that they are at risk . If ninety-nine percent of women back home in my country are circumcised,
what chance does an individual woman stand if she tries
to protect her own daughter from it?'

From Corinna I learn that even under the Geneva
Convention on Refugees the threat of genital mutilation

is not grounds for political asylum. 'Hang on, there's worse to come. The British spokesman went on to talk about another reason and this is even more incredible. He said if FGM was not practised in all parts of the country of origin then it was OK to deport a woman back home. She could move to another part of the country.'

Right, I think. I remember the conversation with Joy. She had told me her family can pursue her even to Europe. What chance would she and her daughter have had if she had just moved to another part of her own country? There are no hard and fast regulations anywhere in Europe. Time and again women are deported who fled their homeland because of the threat of mutilation. And they send them right back to hell.

As I walk home I start to shiver. There are so many supportive and hospitable people living in Europe so why are these women turned away? I had to marry a man I did not love just to be able to get permission to stay in the UK. To this day I have to deal with prolonged bureaucratic delays and lots of red tape if I want to make a journey inside of Europe and then I have to ask my hosts to take on a guarantee for me, saying they are prepared to meet all my expenses during my stay, including any medical costs.

Is it really the case that there is no room for us here?

Sometimes I enjoy the anonymous atmosphere of a small Viennese pub that is a bit run-down but has its own charm. When I go there I will order a typical Austrian speciality and I love to watch the other customers while I eat.

There's a pool table in the middle of the room. A man of about forty, rather full of himself, has just challenged a young woman to a game. Even though she is confident and seems to know what she is doing, the man is being very patronising about telling her the rules and how to hold her cue. Now the other men in the pub are starting to join in and are making cynical comments. I only understand the odd phrase: 'She's up for it!' '. . . can't get the shot in even when he's playing against a woman'.

The young woman stays calm. She puts away shot after shot. The atmosphere grows tenser as the minutes pass. When the woman scores the final point and her eyes flash with triumph, the man looks a bit lost. I can't help grinning, and I laugh at him. Arrogantly he calls out, 'You've got to let a woman win.' The other men nod in agreement.

The young woman tries to save the day by going over to the man with her hand outstretched and saying, 'You are a good loser.'

'That's you told,' I say to myself.

'If I had played my usual game you wouldn't have had a chance,' he says sarcastically. 'That's what we call a special handicap because you're a woman.' His mates drink his health and pat him on the back approvingly.

That is so typical, I think angrily. I look the woman in the eye. I understand all too well what is going through her mind: the feeling that you are not being taken seriously, that you're being discriminated against, that you're being made to look ridiculous – the humiliation of not being respected because you are a woman. I am furious, chuck a few coins on to the table, throw a scornful glance at the men and leave the pub.

Outside on the street there is lots going on. A young woman is laughing with the baby that she pushes along in its pram. Over there a few women wearing headscarves are having a lively debate. The evening sun is nearly gone. The whole scene is bathed in deep red light. Two young men at the street corner are staring at me. Maybe they have recognised me, but I don't care any more. I am still fuming at the stupid chauvinistic attitude of those men round the pool table. Oppression takes so many forms.

What role do men play in the whole issue of FGM? I don't want to hear the argument that genital mutilation is a purely female matter. That is nonsense. After all, we live in a world where the laws are made by men, the religious leaders are men, and the economy is firmly in the hands of the men, i.e. a world where men decide everything. So why should they remain silent on the question of FGM? Many men I have met knew practically nothing about the subject – because they weren't interested. They saw it as their job to preserve traditions and to keep the religious commandments. What this meant in detail they did not really want to know.

I am convinced: If we want to abolish the practice of FGM for ever we are going to need the support of the men. If we can manage to interest them in the issue, we will be a whole lot nearer the goal.

A few days later I went to see Lea at home. She told me about a long chat she had had the previous evening with an African man. 'We talked about FGM as well. It was really interesting.'

Funny. I can't get the question out of my mind – could it be that African men are more prepared to talk about sexuality to a western woman? I am keen to know what Lea learned.

'Cara (not his real name) is thirty-one and comes from Sierra Leone. I have known him for some time. He lives in a privately run hostel for refugees. Yesterday Cara asked me what I was up to and I told him about the FGM research I have been doing for you. First he looked rather put out. I asked him if women were circumcised where he came from – he just nodded and said it was better for having children. He really didn't know what was actually done and how the procedure was carried out, that was women's business. It would show a lack of respect to talk to an African woman about it.'

This lack of communication between men and women – that is exactly the problem. Lea confirms it. 'Cara told me he was taught as a child that it is a mark of disrespect to ask questions. His father had dealt with his childhood curiosity by beating him. Women were an absolute taboo topic anyway. Even to talk about his sisters. He had never talked about "women's matters" with them. He had never slept in the same room as them. Boys and girls were always kept separate.'

'In most African cultures it is a serious offence to show disrespect. If you break the rules your whole life will be unhappy, they think,' I explain to Lea.

'That must be it. Last night I really got the impression that Cara was afraid to talk about it,' says Lea, as she gets some notes she made about their conversation.

'It took about a quarter of an hour for him to start asking questions. For example, he wanted to know what exactly happens when a girl is circumcised. I can still see the shock in his face now when I gave him some details. At first he didn't believe what I was telling him. Especially when I told him about the pain that is involved. He thought that couldn't possibly be true, because African women did have sex and they went on to bear children, too. For that, everything has to work properly.'

Lea had got into the swing of things by now and had warmed up to the subject. She screwed up her face in distaste. 'Do you know what he told me? Sex wasn't important for African women. Sex was just so that children could be born. And that African women would just lie there and let it all happen. European women on the other hand would take an active role in bed.'

These sentences hit me hard. I think about those internet forum sites with the messages from desperate young girls describing their first sexual encounters. How infinitely sad their situation is. How much worse it will be if they come across a man as ignorant of their plight as Cara seemed to be.

When I am sitting on my own in the office a few days later, the door bell goes. I open the door and there's a tall young woman standing there. She is wearing jeans and a tight T-shirt and is carrying a little child that is playing with her gold hoop earrings. I am soon to discover that she has had more experience of life in her seventeen years than most people would pick up in an entire lifetime. Tabea (not her real name) wanted to meet me and her social worker had given her the contact details.

'Waris, you know what it's like. You can't escape the rites, you don't have a chance,' she starts, haltingly. 'Especially when I was little, I thought the ritual was going to be something really fantastic. They tell you that circumcision will turn you into a proper woman and that there'll be a celebration and presents.'

Tabea pauses. We have gone through to the other room to sit and talk. Tabea seems to feel at ease here. She continues her tale.

'My mother woke me up before dawn. When I went downstairs I knew something terrible was going to happen to me. I asked my mother, "Where are we going?" She didn't answer.'

Then Tabea went on to tell me about the circumcision in Somalia. What she tells me reminds me of what happened to me. I put my arm round her and stroke her black curls with my right hand. She is crying and her whole body is shaking. She looks utterly hopeless, crouched there on the sofa staring into a corner of the room. After a while she calms down and goes on with the story.

'I was pregnant and had to run away. My father would have thrown me out if I had had an illegitimate child. And then my family had insisted that if it were a girl, the baby would be circumcised. I thought to myself, I'm not going to let my baby go through what they did to me. I've had terrible pain ever since I was six when it was done to me. I get depressed all the time. And I keep having awful nightmares. I keep dreaming they're coming to get me again. I try to fight them off but it's no good and I end up being taken along with them. Then a woman turns up and I know straightaway she is going to hurt me. I try to defend myself but I can't escape. Usually I wake up feeling absolutely in despair. The dreams are so bad that I'm glad to have woken up.'

'I know the feeling,' I say. 'But at least you have been able to rescue your daughter. How did you get to Austria?'

'It was a terrible journey. First I went to Ethiopia and that's where I had the baby. Then I started on the journey to Europe, stowing away on a ship. We didn't have anything to eat or drink for days. When we got to Italy we had to climb into the back of a lorry and hide between stacks of palettes. It was really cramped and dark and I was terrified we'd be found. Some time later we got to Linz and the man who let me out of the lorry demanded fifteen thousand euros. I was horrified – I didn't have any money – so the man said I would have to work off the debt.

'He forced me to go with him. I didn't have any choice. We drove on until we crossed the border into Bavaria and stopped at a run-down old house. From the outside you couldn't see it was actually a brothel. Downstairs there were two red sofas where the customers would sit and wait until the madame told them which room to go to. She was horrid. Whenever she caught me crying she would say, "Count yourself lucky that you have work here. You're so ugly, you'd never get a proper man, and now you'll have lots of them."

'I had to spend a year in the brothel and had to serve a couple of hundred clients in that period. The men all thought it was a real novelty, having a woman who was circumcised. It seemed to be a real turn-on for them. I had a big room upstairs on the first floor. It had a huge double bed and a wardrobe with a mirror on the door. The plaster was coming off the walls. I just lay there on that bed and let them do it to me, again and again. It didn't make any difference to the men that I was crying. If anything, it excited them. Just the one time there was a young man and he stopped when he saw I was in pain and he apologised to me.'

Tabea swallows hard. The tears are flowing down her cheeks. She has never told anyone about this awful experience before. 'How did you manage to get away?' I ask her in a whisper.

'One day when the Madame slapped me across the face for no reason at all, I made up my mind to get away. One of the regular clients helped me.'

I am speechless. This girl is so young and has had to endure such humiliation. She has gone underground as she has no papers and no hope of ever getting a residence permit. If she goes to the police and makes a complaint against the people who abused her, she and her baby will be thrown out of the country. If she goes public she will be frightened that her family from Somalia will catch up with her – because the traffickers who took her to Europe will know how to put pressure on her.

Suddenly the door opens and my manager, Walter, comes in the room. Tabea cringes in fear. She stands up, quickly says goodbye and heads for the door. I call after her, 'It's only a friend of mine, come to collect something.'

She stops, turns round again and begs me, 'Make it
stop.' And again, 'Please make it stop.'

I would have done anything to help her, but I never
saw her again. I did not know where she was staying and
all my efforts to find her were fruitless.

2

island of the blessed

It is unacceptable that the international community remain passive in the name of a distorted vision of multiculturalism. Human behaviours and cultural values, however senseless or destructive they may appear from the personal and cultural standpoint of others, have meaning and fulfil a function for those who practise them. However, culture is not static but it is in constant flux, adapting and reforming. People will change their behaviour when they understand the hazards and indignity of harmful practices and when they realize that it is possible to give up harmful practices without giving up meaningful aspects of their culture.

Joint statement by the World Health Organization, UN Children's Fund (UNICEF) and UN Population Fund, February 1966.

As a model I often worked in Paris. Maybe that is why I feel so at home here. Or perhaps it is because I do not attract so much attention here merely because I am an African woman. There are parts of Paris where the black population is greater than the white. It makes a welcome change from Vienna. Paris has flair and charms all of its own. As a city it is at once proud and almost unapproachable and yet exercises a strange attraction. The scent of the past, tradition and culture pervades the whole place. The hectic atmosphere in the streets does not prevent me enjoying the time I spend there. I love walking through the streets of the different *quartiers*, looking at the window displays, taking a *café au lait* in the *cinquième* in some pavement café or having lunch in a little bistro on the Rue de Rivoli.

In France the subject of female genital mutilation is talked about more openly than anywhere else. The laws banning the practice are no more stringent than those of neighbouring countries – but one aspect is totally different here: the laws are actually enforced. Abusers are convicted and women are given support. There is a duty on anyone suspecting that the abuse has taken place, be they doctors, nurses or social workers, to notify the authorities. If they fail to do so they are liable to disciplinary action or they can find themselves charged with complicity. They are obliged to start proceedings even if there is only a suspicion that a circumcision is being planned.

An important role in the campaign against FGM is played, of course, by medical staff and social workers attached to the health centres and mother and baby clinics. They are in direct contact with the women and girls affected – the victims or potential victims of the practice. In order to reach as many of these women as possible, treatment and antenatal care is free of charge, and the women who go along to these clinics are not expected to make any contributions to health or social security schemes.

The courts in France are also absolutely clear on the application of the law on this issue: not only the party carrying out the actual operation but also the parents who want their child circumcised are seen as being guilty of committing an offence. They will be brought to court and convicted and they will have to pay compensation to their daughter. That all sounds splendid. So, does that make France a true Island of the Blessed?

I will certainly have to get myself to Paris. I want to see with my own eyes what the situation is like there, and speak to people who are at the forefront of the fight against FGM. I have heard that there is supposed to be a doctor there who has specialised in reconstructing damaged clitorises. He is said to be the only surgeon in Europe involved in work of this nature. I want to find out if such an operation is actually feasible.

I am accompanied by Walter, my manager, by Joanna, the vice-president of the Foundation, and by Julia. I have asked them all to come with me because I am feeling apprehensive, particularly when I think about going to see this doctor. It turns out my instincts are right on this score.

During the flight I have been leafing through the research my team has compiled for me. The most

important facts about France's attitude to FGM are summarised in these papers. I am impressed. They really are
hot on this topic. I learn that a large number of the
Africans in France are from sub-Saharan countries, particularly from Senegal, Mali and Mauritania. In the Paris
region the majority will be from Mali, it seems, but in
France as a whole it is the Senegalese immigrants who
form the largest group. Experts have calculated that in
the whole country around sixty-five thousand women and
girls are already circumcised or at risk.

'It's insane,' I say to Julia, showing her an article from
a newspaper. 'It says here that immigrant families are carrying out genital cutting even if the practice has already
been outlawed for ages in their own countries and is generally disapproved of by people back home.'

'It may be insane, but I'm afraid it's true,' sighs Julia.
'The French sociologist Isabelle Gillette-Fayer tells me
that African people insist even more determinedly on pre-
serving their traditions when they are living abroad.'

'That's right,' I say. 'It doesn't matter if they are in
Paris or in London – they are still isolated from the rest of
society. They will have their own shops, their own clubs,
their own language, their own culture. If you are on your
own in a foreign land your customs from home take on a
special significance.'

I go back to the papers I had been studying and take
one to show something to Walter. The title of the article is
'Recommendations for the total abolition of FGM' and it
was written by a group of scientists working for the
Académie Nationale de Médecine.

Walter finishes reading the text and shakes his head in

disbelief. 'That's amazing. It details exactly how FGM can be successfully combated. I've never seen anything like it.'

'Exactly,' I answer. 'That is what ought to be happening all over Europe. That's what we need to be fighting for.'

A mist shrouds the city when we land at Paris. The temperature is twelve degrees. Not bad for autumn.

I take a taxi to Linda Weil-Curiel's office. She is a lawyer that I have heard a great deal about and she has been campaigning for nearly twenty years to get FGM abolished. Her rooms are on the Place St. Germain-des-Près. It is a name that nearly everyone knows, whether or not they have ever been to Paris. At one corner of the square you have Les Deux Magots, the Left-Bank café where Simone de Beauvoir and Jean-Paul Sartre famously used to hang out. Next door there is a luxury Louis Vuitton boutique; next to that again is No. 6, a typical historic Parisian building with an imposing entrance hall, all deep red carpets and white marble and an old-fashioned wrought-iron lift that takes me up to the third floor.

Each of the rooms in the office suite reflects a different aspect of Linda's professional life: an elegant reception area for the celebrated top lawyer and next to it a small, simply furnished office for the socially committed activist. Shelves full of videotapes ring the room. It is the biggest collection of material about FGM that I have ever seen. It comprises recordings of programmes, talk shows and documentaries on the topic, ranging from Arte to Oprah Winfrey.

The first impression of Linda reminds one of the French film star Annie Girardot. She worked with Simone

de Beauvoir and together with her father represented
Jacqueline Picasso in a court case about Pablo Picasso's
estate. Anyone who is anyone on the cultural scene in
Paris knows her; she is part of the art world and the film
world. If she puts her mind to something she will see it
through to the end. One of her chief projects is to eradicate female genital mutilation in France, irrespective of
whether the actual operation takes place in France itself
or back in Africa.

'Circumcision is mutilation,' she says. 'Mutilation. We
have to say this loud and clear. That's why I don't refer to
it as genital mutilation but as sexual mutilation. The aim
is to destroy the woman's sexuality.'

She sits down at her desk and I take a seat opposite her
on an elegant antique upholstered chair. On the desk are
piles of folders and documents and unopened letters. 'I
can't keep up with the work. I don't know how to manage.
I'm constantly dealing with enquiries from journalists or
students or television companies. I have to turn them
down nowadays because I can hardly get to do the actual
work itself – though somehow or other, I do it, of course!'

With the organisation known as CAMS (Commission
pour l'Abolition des Mutilations Sexuelles) behind her,
she dedicates herself to bringing FGM cases to justice.
Genital mutilation operations have constituted a criminal
offence in France since August 1983 and ever since the
law was passed Linda has been working determinedly to
ensure that it is implemented. She has taken thirty-six
cases to court.

Mostly it will be the parents who face charges. 'It is
practically impossible to lay our hands on the women who

carry out the procedures. Nobody will betray them.'
Relatively speaking it is easier to get the parents convicted. 'The evidence can't be denied. A daughter with
mutilated genitalia – it can't be explained away.'

In the early years after the law came into force convictions usually resulted in probation, but recently judges
have insisted on more severe sentences. This is one of the
things that Linda has been fighting for.

'I am sure if this were being done to little white children there'd be draconian punishments handed out left,
right and centre. Ten, twenty years in jail at least.'

It was in 1993 that the first parent was imprisoned for
this offence.

'What happens to the children when the parents are
convicted?' I ask.

'After the trial they stay with their families,' Linda
replies. 'That way at least the younger children are looked
after. That is the main thing.'

In the courtroom Linda also files a parallel suit in the
name of CAMS and sues for damages for the victims who
are minors.

'That is often harder for them than a prison sentence.
It could be up to 25,000 euros.'

A special fund makes the money available in the first
instance and the parents have to pay off the amount in
instalments. If the girls are still minors, the court appoints
an official to look after the money in the girl's name.

We talk about the court procedure in these cases.

'They all stick to the same absurd story more or less,'
Linda tells me. 'Maybe the mother will claim that she was
out in the park with her daughter and a woman came up

to her and asked her if the girl had "been done".
Sometimes they will say it was in a park, other times on
the street somewhere near where they live, or it might be
in a shopping centre. Or perhaps on a bus. There's very
little variety in the accounts they give. The mother will say
that she answered "no" when asked if the child is circumcised. Then the woman will say, "No problem. I'll do it for
you. It will be quick and clean and nobody will know. Ring
me up if you want my help." A few days later the woman
will turn up at the mother's home, disappear into the
bathroom with the child for a quarter of an hour or so
and then come out saying, "All done." The mother does-
n't know the woman's name or where she's from; she just
knows she is African. When I ask the mother whether she
heard her child screaming while she was being mutilated,
the answer of course is "No". If I ask if the child lost any
blood, she will say, "Oh yes just a few tiny drops. I just
wiped them away with a cloth." It's the same lies every
time.'

'But the judges must realise that the mothers aren't
telling the truth,' I object.

'Not if the judge in question is dealing with the issue
for the first time. If he is not well informed on the subject
he won't know the right questions to ask. The officials
don't realise that not just any African woman can carry
out the sexual mutilations. Or that this is a separate pro-
fession and a woman would have to belong to a certain
caste in order to perform the operation. Everybody in
the woman's circle would know her name.'

'But that stuff about the tiny drops of blood,' I say,
'that's just grotesque.'

'Of course there would be lots of blood,' agrees Linda. 'It is absolutely ridiculous to claim the girl hadn't been bleeding. The genital area is full of blood vessels!' Linda takes a deep breath. 'So the child didn't cry out . . .? Ludicrous. It is a very specific kind of scream. It goes right through you. You could never ever forget what it sounds like.'

'It is like tilting against windmills. After the first few court cases they started to send their girls back to Africa to get them done. But that doesn't stop it being a criminal offence. If you were born in France you are a French national and under the protection of French law at home and abroad. The parents are committing an offence if they send the girl back home for the sexual mutilation.'

'When these cases were brought before the court the parents would say the mutilation had happened without their knowledge. Usually it will be the grandmother that gets the blame. They say she had it done without the parents' consent. If I ask about the granny, she's just died. Seems to be quite dangerous for grandmothers to get visitors from France. They tend to die straight after the visit,' laughs Linda.

'It is of course perfectly possible to have your child go home to Africa for a visit and have her return safe and sound. If you want to ensure her safety you take her to a mother and baby clinic or one of the other welfare centres. You get her examined and a certificate will be issued, stating that she is intact,' Linda explains. 'Then you get an official stamp saying the girl will be re-examined upon her return to France. All sorts of official stamps go on the papers. The mum then goes home with her daughter.

She's now got these papers she can show round in the village and she can tell her family she will be punished if they mutilate the girl. The dad can also send a letter home with them saying he will get sent to prison if his relatives do anything to the girl. That way they can be quite sure their daughter won't be touched. Further, the father is probably sending money home to his relatives, and they'd be stupid to risk cutting off the money supply.'

So far there have been three occasions when charges have been brought in France against the women who carry out the operations; in 1991, 1994 and 1999. One of the women was accused of having mutilated forty-eight girls. Twenty-six sets of parents were charged at the same time. There was huge public interest. The woman was sentenced to eight years, after one of her victims, an eighteen-year-old girl, brought charges against her.

We have been talking now for about two hours. Linda speaks with passion and her anger and emotion are genuine. I know she is on my side: an ally.

'What is your attitude to the organisations that campaign for education rather than pursuing transgressors through the courts?' I ask.

Linda rolls her eyes and now she starts to look impatient, even irritated. 'We have been talking about this for twenty years. For twenty years!' She raises her voice and leans over the desk to look me straight in the eyes. 'And what has been achieved? Nothing. Absolutely nothing at all.' Her expression is scornful as she sits back down in her chair. 'At this rate the practice of sexual mutilation will still be rife here in a hundred years from now! I tell you, the only thing that has had any effect is taking them to court. They understand that. Just imagine, you're living out in one of the suburbs and you want to get your daughter mutilated. What do you think would be more likely to make you change your mind: a few well-meaning women coming and saying, "Of course we respect your culture and we know you just want to do what's right for your daughter", or if you're going to have to be scared the neighbours will see you being carted off in handcuffs?'

Linda does not have much faith in the principle of showing consideration for cultural traditions on this issue. 'Traditions, different values, respect for other people's cultures, that's all well and good,' she says, with a dismissive gesture. 'But we are here in France! People who want to live here have to accept that they are subject to French law and that the law applies to everyone. It's not open to negotiation! If it was white children this was happening to there'd be no FGM by now. But if it's black children, we're to turn a blind eye? It's sheer racism!'

Linda wants quick results. 'If we wait for the majority to be convinced, it'll be a long wait and we mustn't be surprised if nothing changes.' She pauses and then says, 'In history, changes are brought about by the actions of individuals – by individual heroes and heroines.'

I have just met one of them.

My next meeting was with Emanuelle Piet, a doctor who runs the Mother and Child Centres in the Seine-St.Denis *département*. The centres are known as PMI, which stands for Protection Maternelle et Infantile. We are sitting together in the kitchen drinking tea and exchanging views. The small room has a chaotic feel and the walls are painted bright red with that rag technique. There are shelves everywhere in the apartment, full of documents whose labels tell of all the misery that women can experience: forced marriages, child abuse, polygamy. And, again and again, court cases involving FGM.

'I started working in the PMI centres about thirty years ago. I started off right at the bottom of the ladder,' Emanuelle tells me. Now there are 1.4 million people living in the *département*. We give antenatal care and look after the health of children from birth up to the age of six.'

The Seine-St.Denis *département* is a classic example of a working class quarter on the edge of Paris. Workers were housed here in the sixties and seventies in particular those from West and Sub-Saharan Africa. At first it was mainly men, with the women and children following them out later on. 'And from then on we were confronted with the issue of girls being mutilated,' Emanuelle recalls.

At first they tried to combat the practice by attempting to run an education programme to show the families that sexual mutilation was illegal and had serious consequences for the health of the girl, but none of this worked.

'So we made up our minds that we would report instances to the authorities,' said Emanuelle. 'It obviously was not enough to just try and change the women's attitudes to it. There were a number of court cases and from that time on things started to be different. There's only so many times you can tell people that sexual mutilation is illegal and that it is bad. They've always done it and they don't know any other way, so they think it is right.'

'How can women be persuaded?' I ask.

'Each time a woman who has been mutilated comes to see me I ask her if she can remember the day that it happened. If she can remember what it felt like. Many of them have a very clear memory of the actual procedure and how awful it was for them. Then they say, "I don't want my child to go through that." As soon as she remembers what it was like, she is won over. Then you can be pretty sure she won't have her own child mutilated in the same way. If a woman comes in who says she doesn't remember what it was like, that's when I'm really concerned. I ask her if she is thinking of having her child sexually mutilated. In fifteen years I have never come across a woman who has said "yes" to that question. They all say, "No. I know it is against the law in France." They all know it is.'

Emanuelle pours me another cup of tea. She is of delicate build and a quiet woman but she also has a fighting spirit and very clear ideas about her goals. She tells me about an African woman who came to her last year because her husband wanted to send their daughter back to Africa to be mutilated. 'We went to the public prosecutor before whom the father had to appear. "Monsieur, we have a medical certificate that states that your daughter has normal healthy genitalia. If she were to return mutilated from her trip to Africa, you will be going to prison." She got back safe and sound.'

These are the small triumphs that it is worth fighting for.

'Then, for example, there was a little girl who told her teacher, "In the holidays I'm going to go to the country

my mum is from and I'll need to have some days off
school because I am going there for a special celebration
that only girls can attend."' Emanuelle tells me. 'Her
teacher phoned me up and the School Board called the
father in and asked him what sort of a celebration this
would be. Of course the father said, "No, no, of course we
are not going to have her circumcised." To be on the safe
side we had the child examined and announced that she
would be examined again on her return, and lo and
behold, she was fine when she got back.'

'So there are ways to protect the girls,' I exclaimed.
'People have been insisting it was impossible to do anything. Especially that it is not possible to have any
influence on what happens outside the country.'

'Rubbish,' replies Emanuelle. 'First of all, if a judge in
the family court gets the impression that he won't be able
to protect the child properly he can put out an injunction
preventing her from leaving the country.'

'And secondly?'

'And secondly there are some African countries that
have made the practice illegal. FGM is against the law in
the Cote d'Ivoire for example. It can happen that the
public prosecutor in Seine-St.Denis just rings up the
public prosecutor in the Cote d'Ivoire. Then the grandparents get paid a visit and they are told, "You know that
the child is expected to return in good health and intact –
and that is what we expect as well." And that is what happened. There are exceptions of course, but there are
certainly ways we can intervene to protect the child.'

The time races by. It is late afternoon by now. We are
not alone any longer. A young man has joined us. He

looks like an African pop star, wearing jeans and a T-shirt and with his shoulder-length hair carefully plaited. Bafing Kul is a musician. He seems sensitive, shy and vulnerable. Only when he starts to talk about his work does he start to blossom and his eyes start to shine.

Bafing is twenty-eight years old. He comes from Mali and has always written songs whose lyrics promote human rights and social justice. He sings about children in slavery, child soldiers or poverty. When he learned about the cruel ritual of genital mutilation he wrote a reggae number entitled 'Exciser, c'est pas bon' – 'Circumcising girls is not good'. At first the song was heard on the radio all the time for one or two weeks. Then it disappeared from the airwaves. Bafing did not give up; he persuaded a couple of celebrated musicians to perform the song with him. They recorded it together. Once again – radio silence. The stations wouldn't play it.

'In Mali eighty percent of the women have been mutilated,' says Bafing. 'There are religious leaders who preach that in Islam an uncircumcised woman is not pure. It is not true at all. There's nothing in the Koran about it. It's all lies.'

When Bafing wanted to make a CD of his songs he was told, yes you can record a CD but that song has to go. You can sing about anything you want but not about the mutilation of girls. You can't talk about that. It's not done. The pressure grew. He received death threats and people shouted at him in the street. He had to leave the country and managed to get to France. Here he was finally able to record the song.

'For me genital mutilation represents an attack on a

woman; it's violence. It is so completely unfair,' he tells
me.

'Can I hear the song?' I ask. He picks up his guitar
and starts to sing. He has a distinctive voice and the
rhythm is catchy. I sit next to him and join in the refrain.
It is a good feeling. There is a way to get to people's
hearts, I think: music.

When I get up to go Emanuelle says, 'Have another
look at Seine-St.Denis. It's one thing to understand a
problem with your head; it's another thing to feel it in
your heart. You have to see how it came about.'

I nod. 'I'll go tomorrow,' I promise.

It is to be a visit to a different world. Half-familiar, half-
strange. Another planet.

Most of France's African immigrants live in Seine-
St.Denis. Areas like this, on the edge of town, are familiar
sights in many European cities. Every metropolis has its
mini-ghettos, whether it is in London, Berlin or
Stockholm. Practically no one lives here who is not an
immigrant. Most of them are unemployed and have no
qualifications and no future – an explosive mixture.

Seine-St.Denis lies in the north of Paris, on Line 5 of
the metro network, with the station 'Bobigny Pablo
Picasso' at its heart. You take a bus from there to get out
to where the people live. There is a big shopping centre
right next to the station and opposite there is the ugly
public building, the préfecture, a dark block with dark-
ened windows. A lonely tricolour flaps damply in the
autumn wind. The vast cobbled square is empty. High-
rise blocks tower fifteen storeys high into the sky: some of

them a beigey brown, others greyish-white. While I am trying to find out which bus to take I bump into a group of people. Officials from the transport company have blocked all the doors of a bus and they are checking all the tickets as the passengers get out. Nearly all of them are African. Many of them don't have tickets and they will have to pay a fine. The police are standing behind the transport inspectors giving each of the passengers a second going-over; they want to see the residence permits, one of the policemen tells me. Every now and again one of them gets pulled out and taken off to the police station. This is probably the most frequent sort of contact any of these people will experience: coming up against the authorities.

Will they be able to go back to join their families today, I wonder? Or will a couple of them end up being deported because their papers were not in order. I will never know. It is a depressing thought. I go off to find the Mother and Child Centre that Emanuelle told me about. Unfortunately it is closed. The woman doctor who is just locking up gives me the address of another organisation in the area.

Five minutes later I am sitting in the number 234 bus. Again, there are very few passengers who are white. Most of the people are of African descent: old women, families, men in suits coming back from work, youths with jeans too big for them and with silver chains round their necks and their wrists. There are also men and women in brightly coloured traditional robes.

I arrive at a small square surrounded by three-storey blocks of flats. The balconies are crowded with bicycles, footballs, wooden chairs and other bits of junk; some of them have washing hanging out to dry or carpets hanging over the railings. It is not only the housing that is dilapidated; the streets are dirty and unswept. At street level there are one or two shops, the euro equivalent of a pound shop, and next to that the premises of the Self-Help group for immigrant women.

Even before I go in I can hear children's voices. There's a language lesson going on; chairs are crowded close together and a dozen or so children turn to look at me as I open the door. In a tiny office behind this room I can see a small black woman sitting at a desk that is covered with stacks of papers. She smiles at me. It is Eleonore, who runs the centre.

'I should like to talk to you about FGM,' I say.

She makes time for me. Her organisation is there to help women from overseas with no knowledge of the language get a start in society. 'We teach them to read so that they can cope with doing ordinary things like the shopping on their own,' says Eleonore. 'We help them write applications or find work so that they can be independent.'

'What do you do to help protect girls from genital mutilation?' I ask her.

'We run education programmes and go into schools and colleges to talk about it. Two-hour sessions. The children who were born here don't know what FGM is, even if their parents are African. We introduce the topic for all the children, not just the African ones.'

Eleonore tells them all the details. 'The children always listen attentively. There are always a couple of girls who are mutilated. They don't know what a clitoris is, because they haven't got one.'

'But isn't it a terrible shock for these girls when they are confronted with reality in that way?'

'Of course it's difficult for them to understand what has happened. At first they are very shocked. You can tell by looking at them. It's taboo to even talk about sexuality. But then they start asking questions.'

I am reminded of Kadi – the young woman who told me her life story by e-mail. She had never had the chance to talk to others in her situation about what had happened, let alone a chance to talk to trained counsellors.

'How do you find out which girls are circumcised?' I asked.

'By instinct. Some girls will be reticent and draw back when I broach the subject, but others will talk quite openly about it. The ones who clam up have to be encouraged to speak. It isn't easy. If you ask them if they have been circumcised they'll say, "No, I don't know." Then we ask them where they're from and whether they've been home for the holidays. If it's to a country where this cruel ritual is still practised, it's pretty clear.'

'Do the parents know that you go into the classroom?'

'No, they just know there is sex education. It's on the curriculum.'

Eleonore smiles. She smiles all the while we are talking. It is not a fake friendliness that she displays and it is not cynicism. This is a woman who is quite open and straightforward. She drops this into the conversation: 'Incidentally, I am cut, myself.' And then she smiles again. 'It helps the children such a lot that I am cut, too.

It is less of a shock for them if I talk to them about it than if a white person were to discuss it with them. I tell them that I was cut and I explain what the health consequences of it were for me. I tell them, for example, that all my children were born by Caesarean section. I tell them my story and talk about my own experiences. Then the children tell me similar things. "Yes, my mum had a Caesarean, too!"'

It could all be so simple. You can meet the girls in school and explain it all to them without them having to be afraid of their families. But what about the women who are grown up, who live here but never go further from home than the supermarket? The organisation has some ideas there, too.

'We put on sewing classes,' Eleonore explains. 'Of course we don't mention that we are going to educate them about FGM at the same time or they would never turn up. But once they are here and together with other women and we bring up the subject, it just starts tumbling out and they talk and talk and talk.

'Some of them will only just be realising how much they are suffering themselves because of what was done to them. This is an important first step.'

'Do you explain the legal situation to the women?'

'There's no point just talking to them about what the law says, because then their reaction is to say, it is only a law, what do I care about that? My mother was circumcised, my grandmother was circumcised, and I have been circumcised. It's an ancient tradition. Why shouldn't I get my daughter circumcised, too?'

I remember my discussion with Linda and what the

penalty can be for a woman charged with this offence. Are the women really aware of this at all?

'There have been a lot of convictions. We have sometimes collaborated with the court system. But in my opinion it doesn't help to lead a woman away in handcuffs and throw her into prison. It doesn't act as a deterrent. No, what I think is you have to get them talking about it. If we can get them used to thinking about the topic, we have a chance. We need them to be talking about it amongst themselves. The fact that the practice is illegal is good – it will stop a lot of people from trying to get it done here in France. But that's not going to stop them going back home and arranging it there.'

'What is your course of action if you hear about a case of mutilation?'

'Girls are examined when they are at primary school. If a case is seen it is reported to the authorities at once. When the girls are older, it's more difficult. We can't alert the authorities any more or we'd lose the women overnight – they'd never trust us again.'

Eleonore radiates unshakeable optimism. I have been talking to her for two hours and it's just after three o'clock as I say goodbye.

I go and have a look at another part of the outskirts of the city that has the same notorious kind of reputation: La Courneuve. It lies between Paris and the Charles de Gaulle airport. If you fly in and take a train into the centre you pass by whole rows of high-rise buildings, some of them twenty storeys or more, dirty and dilapidated. From the overland station I walk in the direction of the blocks

of flats, passing an enormous supermarket. Just opposite
the supermarket there is a little greengrocer's, run by an
Algerian, in a building put up in the fifties that could do
with quite a bit of repair.

These high-rise flats only house people of African
descent, it appears. According to Eleonore, the families
from Africa simply bring with them the social structures
from back home when they move to France. That's obviously not going to work here. In the villages in Mali, she
tells me, the men all live separately from the women in a
special house. All the men have several wives and each of
the wives has her own hut where she will live with her
children.

In La Courneuve what happens is this: the men put a
few small flats together and their one, two, three or four
wives get put into one of these small flats. The women do
not know each other and may not be able to understand
each other's language; they live there with maybe ten or
fifteen children, all crowded together in the most
cramped of conditions. Often, the women will not be able
to read or write and they have no chance at all of social
integration. The husband comes to see them when he
feels like it.

I look up at the endless rows of windows and wonder
what dramas are being played out behind the walls of
those flats in the high-rises . . .

'There are two important aspects to be considered
when we're dealing with FGM,' Eleonore had told me.
'There's the phenomenon of the polygamous marriage: a
man is obliged to satisfy his wife sexually – it says so in the
Koran. When he has three or even four wives, that's not

going to happen, unless the women have been cut so that sex becomes a painful ordeal for them.'

Living in polygamous marriages is extremely hard for women when they are forced to live crowded together, as they do in these estates on the outskirts of Paris. Eleonore told me they were campaigning to get polygamy made illegal in France. When the law finally came into force, they realised it was the wrong ones who were being hit by it, because the second and third wives ended up losing their residence permits. Some of them had to leave France after perhaps living here for over twenty years. 'They had to go back to Africa – to nothing, nothing at all.'

A problem that is possibly even more important is arranged and enforced marriages. Linda had explained the situation to me, as well. 'I keep hearing about girls who are kidnapped and sold into marriage. Some of it happens here in Europe, some of them get sent back to Africa.' Often it will be a young schoolgirl here, seized out of the everyday world she knows as a French teenager. She will be kidnapped, raped by some stranger claiming to be her husband and then kept captive. But a girl cannot be 'sold' into marriage unless she has been genitally muti-lated. 'That is why the fathers are keen to make sure the girls get "done",' Eleonore explains. Genital mutilation increases the market value of the girl – even in twenty-first-century Europe.

Furiously, I turn away from the blocks of flats. Between the ugly buildings groups of teenagers are sitting around together on the grass. Mothers are walking their babies in pushchairs, children are coming home from school and adults are returning from work. There is loud music coming from speakers set up by some young people who are handing out flyers for a concert by an African singer.

It was obviously part of the original planning to have had shops at ground level in the high-rise blocks. There has been a fire in one of the spaces left and I can only find one single shop that is still functioning. It is quite small and it is crammed with wares from floor to ceiling, including manioc and plantains and lemonade with labels in Arabic script. Behind the cash-desk I can see lots of cosmetic and hair-care products: lotions to straighten and to lighten the hair and to bleach the skin. In front of the shop a young black man is selling roasted corncobs for one euro a bag. He has a supermarket trolley next to him, its chain still dangling, filled with corn on the cob, and with a barbecue tray heaped with hot coals on top of it. I buy a corncob and then ask him where he gets it from.

'From the fields, of course. Where else would I get it?'

'Is that how you make your living, selling that?' I ask in surprise.

'How else?' he snaps back. 'There aren't any jobs. Not for us. Nobody's going to give a black man work here.'

That day I come across maybe a dozen boys with shopping trolleys and corn, doing the same thing. It seems to be the only way to earn any money. No wonder many of the Africans hope to go back home one day. It was like that for Eleonore's father. 'The whole time he has been here, he's never bought even a stick of furniture. He was always saving up to build a house back in Africa. He's been here forty years and now he will never go home. The Africa he has in his head doesn't exist anymore.'

It is no wonder that the immigrants uphold the old traditions, holding fast to the good ones and the bad alike. It is no wonder that the FGM legislation does not reach these people. It seems there is very little of Europe that has reached them at all.

On my way back to the bus stop I notice an old woman in a traditionally patterned blue and white African robe crouching on the ground, gnawing away at a corncob. She could have been in my village back home. She looks as if she has been beamed in from another world. Behind her, instead of savannah, there are rows of bus shelters made of dirty, scratched Plexiglass; in front of her the traffic thunders past. If Europe really wants to combat the practice of FGM, I think, something needs to be done to give women like this some sort of a chance. They should be given education, equal rights and, most importantly, respect. As long as they have no possibility of integration into our society, they will cling fast to whatever they bring with them from home.

I go back to the hotel, deep in thought. St-Denis and La Courneuve are nothing but ghettos, places that are neither Europe nor Africa. Small continents of their own, with their own laws.

I am feeling apprehensive. Today is the day of my appointment with the man thousands of circumcised women are pinning their hopes on: his name is Dr Pierre Foldès and he has developed a surgical technique which he claims can rebuild a missing clitoris.

Is it really possible? Will he be able to help me? Do I really want him to help me?

The taxi weaves in and out of the traffic round the Place Charles de Gaulle at the Arc de Triomphe and drives down the Avenue Grande Armée. Walter and Julia have come with me and they can sense my unease. We go through tunnels, pass the grubby apartment blocks on the outskirts and leave the city on the motorway heading north-west. After about half an hour we turn onto a road leading to the idyllic St-Germain-en-Laye, with its forty thousand inhabitants, small honey-coloured houses, tiny winding streets and a twelfth-century castle where Louis XIV, the Sun King, was born.

The hospital is clearly signposted and the taxi takes a steep narrow road up to a complex with several low build-ings, where it stops and we get out. There is a chilly wind and the clouds are hanging low.

Dr Foldès has his consulting room in one of the small hospital buildings. He is said to have operated on about three hundred women and there are hundreds of women on the waiting list for surgery. He is the only surgeon doing this operation but he is currently said to be training others in the technique. I start to feel very uneasy. I have been so looking forward to meeting this man, but now I am getting butterflies about the visit. The matter I am consulting him on is the most personal and intimate one possible, my clitoris, one of the parts of my body that were simply cut away. It is about my sexuality.

Dr Foldès is waiting for us and I feel relief when I see him. He is a tall, grey-haired man with a reassuringly calm manner, and greets me with a warm smile. He looks a bit like a TV doctor. I start to feel more confident.

The surgery is small and well-lit, with an examination couch next to the door. On the wall above it are two large frames with lots of photos from Africa. They are not pretty pictures: shots of half-starved children, young boys with appalling injuries to arms or legs, blood, doctors operating, and examples of limbs displaying obvious signs of disease.

Dr Foldès invites me to take a seat. 'I am a surgeon and a urologist,' he says, 'and I am also the doctor responsible for Asia on the Doctors for the World committee. I started specialising in the treatment of women in Burkina Faso twenty-five years ago. In France we now have a technique for rebuilding the clitoris. The procedure is recognised by the Académie Nationale de Médecine and by the French state health insurance scheme.

'The method is relatively straightforward,' continues Dr Foldès. 'We remove the scar tissue and expose the healthy section of the clitoris that still remains even after mutilation has taken place. The clitoris itself is very long, about eleven centimetres, and most of it is totally hidden under the scar.'

I am amazed. So the clitoris is still there after all? 'But some types of mutilation remove the clitoris completely, don't they?'

'Part of the clitoris will always be preserved. The mutilation leaves a thick scar and the heavy bleeding caused by the cut will fill the cavity and push the rest of the clitoris back inside. So, when we surgically remove the scar tissue we find the healthy tissue underneath with healthy nerves and blood vessels. Then we can reconstruct the clitoris.'

'How long is the operation?'

'About an hour and a half.'

Just ninety minutes, and then everything is back to normal? Is it really so simple to get rid of all the pain and the shame, the humiliation and trauma, that I have been carrying with me all these years? This doctor is sitting there giving the impression it is all a matter of simple surgery. I am lost for words. The feeling of deep unease is starting to return. I shudder at the thought of ever again letting anyone near me with a sharp instrument, a scalpel, a pair of scissors, letting them touch the wound again.

Haltingly, I put my questions. 'As a woman who has gone through genital mutilation . . . the thought of undergoing the same thing again . . . is horrendous. And then, on the other hand, the thought of having a function restored that was stolen from me . . . What is it like for the women who have had the operation? Do they come back . . . ?'

'It is vital you come back. Patients are seen four times: after two weeks, after four weeks, after six months and then a year after the operation. This is important, and helpful for the women.'

'Helpful? Yes, it must be. Because they will be having feelings they have never experienced before.

'A whole team of people is there during this stage of recovery to support the women. They don't come back to me but to see a psychiatrist and a sex therapist My team reports that these women are discovering feeling again after their operations. By my reckoning this is the case for about eighty percent. We are doing a scientific study that is not finished yet.'

Eighty percent? So the operation does not work for every woman, but for most of them it does. They get back what they lost. I am starting to feel hope. My voice sounds quite cheerful as I ask if we may take a look at the work he does. This turns out to be a mistake.

'Of course,' answers Dr Foldès. 'What would you like to see?'

'I want to see everything, the whole operation, from beginning to end and what it looks like afterwards.'

'I can show you a video that demonstrates it all quite well, I think.'

Against a dark background you see a diagram of a woman's body in section. Two thick round cords run back from the place supposed to represent the vagina, running in parallel towards the back and then separating to left and right. 'This shows a normal clitoris. You can see it is much longer than the part of it normally visible,' Dr Foldès explains.

The video goes on to show these two cords cut away in front. 'This is what happens in a genital mutilation. In areas of western Africa and in East Africa they tend to cut away more than that, up to here.' Dr Foldès points on the screen. I feel faint.

He goes on. For him the operation is a technical procedure. He is explaining his craft. It could just as well be a diagram of the workings of a car engine. But this affects me deeply and I can't just pretend I'm listening to a description of the function of a cylinder head or how to repair faulty suspension.

'We always have the same initial situation.' The doctor's voice seems to come from somewhere far away. 'We've got the nerves here, in yellow, and we cut away the scar to expose the healthy part of the clitoris.' He waves his hand, points to the screen and demonstrates exactly what happens. Another bit of the cords disappears.

'Here we have to lengthen them. So we make a small incision in these "bands", and the bands give and the cords slip down a little. In this way we can make the clitoris longer and bring it back to correct position together with its nerves.' He means the place where the outer section of the clitoris had been before the circumcision cut it away. On the screen the cords extend towards the front. All done.

'Uh . . . I . . . how . . .' I don't know what I am trying to say. My enthusiasm has disappeared. I feel empty. I feel nothing at all. It all looks so artificial, viewed on the screen like that. It bears no similarity to a real human body. 'Um . . . How do you make the clitoris longer?' I ask, just for something to say. My head is going round and round. It does not seem real at all. The light coming through the rather grubby little window is starting to fade. In a cramped dark office we are staring at a small dark screen that has grey and yellow threads moving around on it.

'We don't stretch it, we just make that little cut in the bands. Hang on, let's look at that bit again.' He moves his fingers on the keyboard to locate the right image and starts to speak again.

'Doctor!' I interrupt him. 'Doctor!'

'Yes?' He looks at me, surprised. I can see from his expression that he was not expecting to be interrupted.

'You know, Doctor, this is all very difficult for me,' I whisper. 'We're sitting here talking about it, but for a woman like me . . . it's very difficult. For any woman, I think. It's about feelings, sensations.'

'Of course,' says Doctor Foldès, turning away from the computer to face me, his hands together on the desk in front of him, expectantly.

I calm down and look at him closely. He is in his mid-forties and he still looks youthful despite the grey hair. I can imagine how he must have looked as a boy. I cannot work out his expression. I do not know if he can understand what is going on in my mind. I think he is just waiting for me to go on. Can he have any idea what it is like for a woman, to have been mutilated in this way?

A determined light comes into his eyes. It is as if he is never going to waver from a course of action he has decided on. Suddenly I feel a wave of gratitude towards him, and almost involuntarily I stammer, 'I admire you for the work you do as a doctor.'

He hesitates, looking at his hands. 'Thank you,' he says finally, with a quick smile and goes on, 'You know it really does help. The scar has no feeling, of course, because the nerves have been severed. But behind that part the function is still there. We found that out in experiments using electric stimulation. I have some photos of how the operation is done, if you would like to see.'

'Yes,' I say, though I am far from sure that I do want to see.

Dr Foldès brings the pictures up on the screen to show the vagina of a black woman, completely mutilated, 'infibulated'. The clitoris and the inner and the outer labia have all been removed, the bloody remains of the flesh sewn up. Afterwards there is nothing but smooth skin with a central scar and a small opening. No hair, no genitalia, nothing. A familiar picture. It makes me feel weak.

The next picture shows the scar cut open to show the red flesh beneath the black skin. Then you see forceps pulling at this flesh, then something being cut off with scissors.

The blood is swirling round in my head and I can hear my heart thumping madly. My face feels hot and I am finding it difficult to get my breath. From somewhere far away I can hear his voice: 'This is the old part of the clitoris that we have to cut off to lay the healthy tissue with the nerves intact.'

I find myself back in my village in Africa, Little Waris in her village again. I can see my sister. I am hiding so I can watch her 'big day' in secret. I hear her cry out, see her kicking and jumping up covered in blood, trying to get away from the women who have sat down on top of her. I can see my mother as she bends over, me holding my body tight as the old woman starts cutting away between my legs. I feel the sudden terrible pain and the unbelievable helplessness, at the mercy of these people who are doing the worst thing in the world to me. I feel the urge to scream, to drive away the image of this excruciating experience, to drive away these pictures I have had inside me for over thirty years and which will not let me rest.

But no scream comes. Instead I start to sob. Dr Foldès stops talking and looks concerned. 'Please . . . where is the toilet?'

He points to the door. 'Just over there.'

As I get up, my legs are shaking. When I get to the toilet I let the tears out. I sit on the toilet seat, my head in my hands, and I cry and cry. My whole body is shaken by the sobbing. I feel so cold.

Then I am sick. Once, twice, three times.

It is as if the ancient scar has been torn open again and is bleeding afresh, bleeding more than ever. I am overcome by pain and sadness. It amazes me that these feelings have resurfaced so vividly.

I do not know how long I have been sitting here. Perhaps five minutes, perhaps half an hour. At last there are no tears left. I manage to open my eyes and take my hands away from my face, looking at my long narrow fingers. They are the fingers of a grown woman, still young, but mature. The sight reassures me. I am no longer that young girl and I am no longer in Africa. I am here in France, in the hospital in St-Germain-en-Laye, and I am here because I want to prevent that same awful thing happening to other girls.

Slowly my strength comes back. I wipe the tears off my face, blow my nose, take a deep breath and open the door. Dr Foldès has turned off the computer again. For something to say, I ask, 'Who pays for the operations?'

'The French state health insurance scheme covers part of the cost. But the operation costs far more than the insurance contribution. We finance the rest ourselves here. I do not want women to have to pay for the operation. For the women it is free.'

Dr Foldès replies calmly to my questions as if nothing had happened. He does not refer to my tears. I am grateful that he does not mention it. Somehow I manage to bring my mind back to the conversation.

'Do the women have to undergo more than one operation?'

'No, it is a single operation.'

I get up and hold out my hand. 'Thank you, Dr Foldès.'

He smiles and nods. As we leave the hospital, the cold wind blows in my face. I feel better now. I breathe deeply.

Life has me back.

The night is a disaster. Back in my hotel room, memories crowd in and my life flows over me like a huge wave. From one moment to the next it seems everything has changed. I sit motionless on the bed and can speak to no one. Then I start to feel giddy again and I am sick once more. I have eaten nothing since the morning.

Walter and Julia look after me in the most touching way. They are concerned about me. I am often moody and unpredictable, but they have never seen me like this before. I have never felt like this before . . . At long last they manage to persuade me to take a sedative and try to get some sleep. It knocks me straight out.

But the demons have not gone. They creep into my dreams, conjuring up all the images from the afternoon. I am in Somalia, in the desert, running away from my father. Or lying on the ground in agony, the day after the mutilation. Voices calling, 'Waris, Waris!'

When I look at myself in the mirror the next day I am horrified. But my body has recovered somewhat and I can eat a few mouthfuls.

I have made a decision: I need to get away from here and I need to get away now. Today. I need room to breathe. I need time to think. I have to get my feelings and my thoughts sorted out. This trip to Paris has really shaken me up. It has made the topic of female genital

mutilation a very personal issue for me. I have entered
the ring and spoken to the victims, telling them, 'You are
not alone. We are fighting this together.'

I tell Walter and Julia of my decision. They have been
expecting it. But Paris will see us again. Linda rang up in
the morning. She must have heard something, and has
rung to ask how I am. She has some news, as well: there is
a new trial starting at the end of November, with the parents of a seven-year-old answering the assault charges. She
wants us to come and observe the court proceedings.

I agree to come. You start something, you see it
through.

3

'it has got to stop;
it just has to stop'

I cannot forget the work Dr Foldès is doing. I keep wondering if he is doing us a favour. Can it really help women like us? I want to speak to others about it. More, I *need* to talk.

Corinna has an idea and suggests going to London to see a midwife who is said to have a great deal of experience with this reconstructive surgery. Her name is Comfort Momoh. Corinna thinks I should really get to meet her.

London! My heart welcomes the sound of the name. London was my first port of safety in Europe. When my uncle, a diplomat, had to flee Somalia, London was my first refuge. I worked in the Somalian Embassy, and during the first years I rarely left the building. When I moved to a student hostel, I was taken on at McDonald's for casual work and then I was discovered as a model. The world I got to know then was a quite different one. London has always been one of my favourite cities.

London, here I come.

Great Britain is not like France. Things are not so clear-cut on this side of the Channel. Of the sixty million inhabitants, about two million are foreigners. Surprisingly few, I think. A little over three hundred and fifty thousand come from Sub-Saharan Africa, from Somalia, Ethiopia, Nigeria, Sudan, Kenya and Mali. There are no figures available about the numbers from the individual countries. When a census is conducted there are questions about ethnicity and skin colour, rather than country of origin, e.g. categories such as 'Black Caribbean', 'Black African' or 'White African'. I do not understand why they do this. What is the point of dividing us up according to the colour of our skin? We are all just people.

London is the UK city with the greatest number of immigrants, but FGM is also an important issue in Manchester, Liverpool, Cardiff and Sheffield. In Cardiff, where I spent two years, there are around twenty thousand Somalis. The organisation that is most active in campaigning against FGM, a group called *Forward*, calculates that about eighty thousand women living in the UK are affected by it. Of course there are no exact statistics. Mutilations are inflicted on girls who were born here or who grew up in this country. About seven thousand are thought to be presently at risk. For the most part the circumcision procedures are carried out back home; nobody

knows the numbers of operations taking place in the UK. A
thousand? Three thousand? Fewer? More? No idea. But all
the groups involved are certain that FGM is practised in the
UK, just like in all the other European countries. In secret,
of course. Names of midwives, doctors or untrained medical workers are passed round by word of mouth. Everyone
knows it is against the law, but the crimes hardly ever come
to light. What is more, there does not seem to be any
system of protecting girls. The general public do not have
to register with the police and there are no compulsory
physical examinations.

Why do Africans cling on so resolutely to this cruel
practice? Perhaps because there are so many social groups
here in the UK, living side by side. Rich ones here, the
poor there. Black here, white there. That will be the same
in other European countries. But in France a big effort is
made to integrate the immigrants, at least formally, with
anyone born on French soil being automatically a French
citizen, whereas the children of Pakistanis, Indians or
Somalis who are born in the UK will stay Pakistani or
Indian or Somali. Even if someone has been living here
for forty years they won't necessarily think of themselves
as British. Integration? Anything but.

Against a background like that tradition plays an
important role in the community. Tradition gives a sense
of identity. African women do not want to be told how to
live by 'Whites'. Most of the Whites exhibit very little
respect for the dignity of Africans. Nevertheless, the
United Kingdom was one of the first countries to react to
the issue of FGM. The legislation is clear. But laws alone
will not solve the problem.

FGM was officially outlawed in England back in 1985 when the Female Circumcision Act came on to the statute books. It was the first law of its kind and makes it a criminal offence either to carry out the procedure or to be an accessory. In March 2003 an amendment was passed that makes it illegal for families to arrange for the procedure to take place back in their country of origin. At the same time the penalty was increased from five to fourteen years' imprisonment. Has it done any good? No. The Act has proved to be a paper tiger. To this day not a single conviction has been made, although it is generally accepted that the number of incidents is rising continually. It is difficult to believe: not a single case has come through the courts. I am determined to find out why.

In Britain as elsewhere, FGM is a taboo subject, especially amongst those who are themselves affected. African women are ashamed to go to a gynaecologist. They do not go until just before their wedding (they go then because otherwise they would risk being opened up on the wedding night with a knife) or before a birth or in a case of a severe problem such as a fistula, menstruation difficulties or extreme discomfort on passing urine. There are now special clinics such women can attend; if they can get over their shame, they can be helped.

One of the best known doctors is the gynaecologist Harry Gordon, who was a consultant at Central Middlesex Hospital in London. He has now retired, but still runs the African Well Woman Clinic that he founded together with the organisation *Forward*. He was the first doctor offering reconstructive surgery for circumcised women. I am sorry I cannot meet him, but I can get to visit the

African Women's Clinic that Sarah Creighton runs.
Working with her assistant Maligaye Bikoo, the gynaecologist Sarah Creighton operates there two days a month,
doing reconstructive surgery for women who have been
infibulated. She has also set up advice centres in the communities.

It is past midnight. I am wide awake. Reading through
the research these last three hours about the situation in
England has shown me the country in a new light. I lived
here for several years but I had not been aware of most of
this material. I used to be part of the African community
in London. I know the other side of the picture. I know
what it is like to live isolated in a country where you do
not speak the language or understand the customs. I
moved in a world full of taboos; subjects like genital mutilation or reconstructive surgery were never mentioned,
could not possibly ever be mentioned.

A twist of fate and my own obstinacy got me out of the
ghetto, but I still feel close to the thousands of African
women who did not manage to get out – who have not yet
managed to get out. It is possible to break out of harmful
traditions. My African sisters are strong and they can
defend themselves.

The sunshine has conjured smiles on to many of the
faces. There is a smile on my face too. I am on my way to
the African Women's Clinic, near the university in one of
the side streets. There's a tiny sign showing that there is a
clinic located in the six-storey building. Here women are
given a portion of quality of life, a little self-esteem.
Reconstructive surgery can be done quite quickly.

Sometimes it only takes ten minutes. The psychological effects take much longer to deal with.

The entrance is narrow, the walls could do with a coat of paint. I ask the security guard, a big black wardrobe of a man, where I can find Maligaye Bikoo. She has a specialist nursing qualification and runs the clinic together with Sarah Creighton. It is a clinic day today and all afternoon women will be coming here for advice. Some will have treatment. The porter sends me up to the fourth floor.

The hospital consists of several buildings connected by a confusing warren of tunnels. It's a long walk. You go up the stairs then down some more stairs, and there is a new world round each corner. Suddenly I am in a sparkling clean reception area and then I get sent up another set of steps to find a tiny office where Maligaye Bikoo is sitting. The room is crammed with papers, piles of boxes, dolls made of material. Maligaye comes from Mauritius and I like her straightaway. She has a ready laugh and looks so enthusiastic that it is catching. Her gestures are generous and she seems secure in herself and has a modest manner.

The women who come to see Maligaye and Sarah Creighton are not the sort who would think of going to a GP or a 'normal' hospital clinic. 'Ninety-nine percent of our patients want to have the reconstructive surgery done under local anaesthetic here in our clinic, so they can keep it secret. If they go to a normal hospital, people will find out. You would have to stay in overnight,' Maligaye tells me. 'These women have to be sure that their families aren't going to find out.'

'Do they always come here on their own?'

'Some do, but some come with a girlfriend or with their partner,' answers Maligaye. 'Especially if the man has been living in England for some time. Lots of men support their women in going for reversal surgery. They are against FGM but they know that it is still the custom in the community.'

'What operations are carried out here?' I ask.

'Mostly we treat women who have been infibulated. First we discuss it with the women at length and explain in detail exactly what will have to be done. If they agree to the reconstructive surgery (de-infibulation) they will have to fill in a permission form. Then we give them some brochures and other leaflets about FGM. During the operation we remove the scar tissue and sew the wound up neatly. It's called a reversal, but it isn't really exactly what we do. If the clitoris has been cut off, of course we can't put it back.'

I want to know more details and make up my mind to ask the midwife Corinna has told me about, Comfort Momoh, whom I will be meeting tomorrow at her home. Since seeing the pictures that Dr Foldès showed me in Paris, I do not suppose anything will shock me anymore, but to be on the safe side I feel I would rather talk about intimate matters in more intimate surroundings.

'What sort of women come here?' I ask instead. I learn that most of the women who attend come when they are about to marry, to have an opening made. Some of the patients, on the other hand, are already married and come because normal intercourse is impossible. Many come because they are pregnant and need an operation to enable them to give birth safely. About eight to twelve women are operated on each month, while a far greater number of women come for advice and information. Treatment is free under the NHS.

The Clinic's work is well known in the community and its reputation is based on word of mouth recommendations. 'On Monday we saw a woman who had come back to us after having had the operation. This time she'd brought her younger sister along with her, to get the same treatment.'

Whenever she can, Sarah Creighton spends time on her research projects. So few scientific studies have been done on FGM. 'We are looking at the symptoms women have before and after the operation we do – difficulty passing water, gynaecological problems,' Maligaye explains. 'The women are asked whether they are willing to be included on the study and if they agree, we put a series of questions to them before, and again four weeks after, the operation.'

The biggest problem is the occurrence of so-called flashbacks. At the time of the operation many patients re-live the trauma of the original mutilation for a second time. 'That's exactly what happened to me in France,' I exclaim. 'I was just listening to the doctor talking through the technical side of the operations and it set me off. Suddenly I could recall every detail of what was done to me as a child that day when they cut me up.'

'Yes,' agrees Maligaye. 'Lots of women get that. They go through it all again, seeing it as if they are watching a film of themselves being mutilated when they were younger. This happens to women who have had apparently no memory of the event until that point and had not allowed any of the pain to resurface, or who could only recall the experience in a fragmentary way or who had only the vaguest of ideas about what had been done to them. All of a sudden it all comes flooding back – right in the middle of the operation. We have a psychologist here on the team and she is able to help the women through this.' For many it will be the first time they will have been able to talk to anyone about their traumatic experience.

It is midday when I leave the African Women's Clinic. London's familiar damp, murky climate has reasserted itself. It is drizzling again. That could be the reason why, besides me, nobody out there on the streets seems to have a smile on their face. What I have found out talking to Maligaye has raised my spirits again; it is a bit like having passed an exam. I feel I failed my first test, back in the Paris consulting room with Dr Foldès. But I have just sailed through the re-take with flying colours.

I know why, as well. In France I had felt part of a scientific experiment to see how well something can be reconstructed after it has been removed. It had seemed that the technical side was more important than the emotional component. Here, in the African Women's Clinic, the patient, the woman, is at the centre of things. Here they concentrate on what will help *her*. She will be given the psychological support that she needs. And that is the way it should be.

*

Comfort Momoh is the FGM specialist midwife. She gives advice to women who have been victims of genital mutilation, supervises their care when they are pregnant or, if they come in to the clinic because of gynaecological problems, helps them with their day-to-day problems. In the course of her career she has re-opened the genital areas of over a thousand infibulated women.

She lives out in one of the London suburbs and it seems to take forever to get there. I go past rows of little brick houses, uphill, downhill, through the middle of a wood, and then finally arrive at my destination. There are lots of small family houses with little gardens in front, and the centre of the estate looks like a village green. The weather is cold and damp.

Comfort is waiting for me in the living room of her home, which is typically furnished with a three-piece suite, a TV and a dining table, and has frilly curtains at the window. She has pictures from Nigeria on the walls, showing scenes of modern-day Africa. Her children are in the playroom watching television. We sit at the table and start to talk. Comfort is a small woman with wild black hair standing out round her head and she has large dark expressive eyes. When she speaks she uses her whole body to underline what she is saying and her voice is telling you that she knows what she is talking about. Her tone is pragmatic.

The reconstructive surgery she carries out at the clinic is not like the operations Dr Foldès was describing. It consists only of cutting open the mutilated scar tissue. Of all the women worldwide who have undergone genital mutilation, about fifteen percent are infibulated, but in

Somalia or Sudan the figure rises to nearly ninety-nine percent. As there are so many women in the UK who come from those areas, the treatment is now fairly routine here.

Comfort explains the procedure to me: 'If a woman has been infibulated, the outer and sometimes the inner labia are sewn together in the middle.' On a piece of paper she does a quick sketch of a vagina with a line lengthways in the middle. 'There's only the tiniest of openings, sometimes no bigger than the head of a match, for the urine and the menstrual blood to find their way out, drop by drop.' She goes on, 'This is where the vagina is sewn up and this is the bit I open up. All this round here is scar tissue. The cut we do will hardly bleed and there should not be much pain because the nerves to the scar are damaged. The edges of the cut are stitched to prevent them growing together again. We tell the women how important hygiene will be after the operation because we find that some women were so traumatised by their previous experience that they are unable to touch themselves there.'

Comfort knows from experience that from a medical viewpoint this reconstructive surgery is a relatively minor procedure. 'The whole thing will take about ten minutes, twenty at the most,' she tells me. 'Then there is a follow-up talk and the women can be out of the clinic after less than an hour in all. It is done under local anaesthetic.'

I am surprised. So, just ten minutes are all it takes to change these women's lives and improve things for them to such an extent. But only a handful of women know about the possibility. A tiny handful.

The midwife tells me that she first became interested in FGM fifteen years earlier. 'I was still doing my training. Where I was there was a large Somali community.' Today she is the only midwife in Britain to hold a specialist qualification in FGM treatment. 'You need to be extremely sensitive and tactful in this job. You can't see things in isolation: we have to work holistically. For some of the women FGM won't be the main issue, and certainly not the only problem they're confronted with. They may be refugees who have just arrived from Africa and they're applying for asylum. They don't speak the language and have nowhere to stay, have no family here and have no idea how they are going to be able to support themselves.'

'What sort of thing can you do to help them?' I enquire.

'When a woman comes here to see me I ask about general things first of all. I ask her where she's from and how long she will be in London, and so on. I give her all the contact addresses she might need for women's support groups in the community, for example. Then I tell her about the legal situation. I tell her about child protection, because most of them have no idea of this. I ask her if she is intending to get her daughters circumcised. Most of them say, "Are you joking? Never in a million years!" Yet again, others are hesitant, and they wonder whether they'll be able to resist the pressure from the family.'

I want to know if she thinks the African attitude to FGM has changed in the UK recently.

Comfort thinks carefully, 'I am sure it has. There's a lot

happening. Five or ten years ago the women who came to
see us were ones just about to marry and wanting the
operation for that reason. Nowadays we have girls coming
in for the treatment because they realise that they are different from western women in this respect and they ask
me to put it right. "Comfort, just do it for me. I want to
feel right again."'

I tell Comfort about my visit to Dr Foldès, and she
nods. 'I am sceptical about that,' she says. 'I am absolutely
sure his intentions are excellent, but I don't think further
cutting away right inside is a good idea. Why cause further
injury? We do the simple version of the procedure, just
slitting open the scar where it was stitched up. The vagina
hasn't changed, as people might think: inside everything
is the same. But overnight they have lost the physical
symptoms that have been plaguing them. With our simple
operation they don't have to pin enormous hopes on
growing a new part of their bodies.'

The physical side is only one aspect. 'Many of the girls
who come here are under tremendous emotional stress. I
try to do my best to help them. Specialists often think
everything will be sorted after the operation, but they are
overlooking the fact that these young girls will need a lot
of support. They need information, respect and a gentle
approach.'

I remember Maligaye telling me yesterday about the
flashbacks that can occur during the operation, making
the woman burst into tears.

'That's why the advice sessions are vital,' says Comfort
in agreement. 'I show the women pictures before we go
ahead, so they know not to be shocked how different

everything looks when there's not just a tiny hole but all open again. Some of them are upset and think it's ugly and they are afraid that their husband won't like it and won't enjoy sex if the vagina is not tightly stitched anymore. They are frightened he will leave them. I try to help the women come to terms with their new body.'

Comfort is on call round the clock. Any patient who asks is given her phone number and can ring her up when they want to speak to her. 'I don't mind that. I know there aren't many clinics for these women to go to.'

'Do you think people in this country are just as ignorant as elsewhere about FGM?' I ask her.

'Absolutely,' says Comfort. 'Even nursing staff, midwives and doctors. There are still doctors who might tell their patients they will have to have a Caesarean if they have a baby. This is nonsense. The vagina is not reduced in size by FGM. Obstetricians and midwives must be told this. It is just the scar line that must be cut open, and there you are. Inside, everything is just the same. A lot of GPs seem to have no idea about FGM, so they are unable to diagnose the symptoms for conditions it may cause. If a woman goes to a doctor complaining of pain when she urinates, she will just be prescribed antibiotics. Even if she goes back four times with the same thing she'll still be given antibiotics again because it won't have occurred to the doctor that infibulation is the cause. A great number of women are in great pain during menstruation because the blood can't escape properly; sometimes the woman gets cysts of all sizes. Others come here with their partners because of problems with intercourse . . .'

'How late can this operation be left when a woman is

pregnant? Can it be done when she's just about to give birth?' I ask.

'Yes, it can be done then, but I would recommend that it is done during earlier stages of the pregnancy. The best time would be about the twentieth week, because if it is done very early on and she has a miscarriage she is bound to feel that's why she lost the baby.'

'Have there been any women who ask to be sewn up again after they've given birth?'

'Hardly ever. I've been working at the clinic for eight years now and I've only come across two women who asked for that to be done. That's why I think it is very important to tell them these things right at the start before I operate: it would be illegal to sew them up. I have to say to them, "When we open the scar here, we will not be able to close it up again." Women need to have this information before labour starts.'

That's strange. We were just talking about exactly that when I was getting ready to fly to England the other day. I had heard that in German hospitals they sew the women up again after they give birth because otherwise they lose too much blood. I take the opportunity of asking Comfort about this.

Quick as a flash comes her answer: 'People who do that have just got no idea. I do three or four of these minor reconstructive de-infibulation operations every week and I know what I'm talking about. There's very little loss of blood. Many doctors are nervous that a woman will lose a lot of blood when the scar is opened up whereas in fact most of them don't bleed at all. The massive blood loss can occur at the time of the circumcision, and that's when many of the victims die. But when the scar is opened up again there is hardly any loss of blood. It is a nonsense, sewing them up again after childbirth. It makes me furious. Just think what that would mean for the average African woman who might have six children. By the time she's been opened up and then closed up again each time, there'd be nothing left of her, she'd be a complete mess.'

For a while we are silent. It is an uncomfortable silence.

'Aren't there any laws about it then in Germany?' Comfort finally asks.

I tell her they do not have specific FGM legislation but that it is covered by laws on bodily harm.

'That has got to be changed. If we are going to define FGM as mutilation, then sewing a woman up again means continuous further mutilation. Again and again.'

My head is swimming after this visit, but I have made up my mind that I am going to do something about it and that I have to make this scandalous practice in Germany public.

I did not realise at the time that it would just be the tip of the iceberg.

Today I am going to see a woman I met via my website. She is keen to meet up because she wants to join in the campaign against genital mutilation. When I give her a ring on the spur of the moment, Bashra (not her real name) asks me to come round to see her. 'I can't get away to meet up in town,' she says. 'I've got the children here.'

I stand at her front door in a typical neat little English suburb where all the streets are laid out symmetrically and the gaps between the buildings are all just so and the trees are all the same distance apart. The houses are identical and the gardens are all the same, as well. It reminds me of the Lego towns my son Aleeke loves playing with. Next door to Bashra men are working on repairing some guttering; their machines make an infernal noise.

An African woman welcomes me shyly. She is quite small and slim and she is wearing a grey robe and a grey scarf on her head. 'We spoke on the phone,' I say in greeting. 'I am Waris.' She nods and smiles; there is a little girl standing behind her, staring at me curiously. 'I didn't think you'd be here so soon. I've just got to take the little one to kindergarten,' she says.

I ask her if I can go with them. Bashra seems quite nervous. It takes quite a time before we get talking properly. She tells me about her children, about the neighbourhood and about her life here in England. Bashra is from the Sudan and came here five years ago as a refugee with her husband. 'Most of the people here won't even return my greeting if I say hello,' she says indignantly. She would love to be in the centre of London where there are more Africans living and the atmosphere would be more open and welcoming. Friends in the neighbourhood? Not a chance.

We arrive at the kindergarten and Bashra kisses her daughter goodbye before we turn round and head back to her house. She has a worried look on her face. 'Sometimes I'm afraid that the other children will refuse to play with her because she's black.' When she asks her child in the evening who she has played with at kindergarten the answer is usually 'With Karin'. But Karin is the name of the nursery teacher.

We are back in the living room in Bashra's home and she is making tea. 'Waris, I want to fight against genital mutilation,' she says suddenly as she comes in with the tea tray. It makes me smile. This tiny woman is looking very determined, and has lost her shyness. 'I so long to be able to speak to another woman the same thing happened to.' Her face takes on a worried, frightened expression.

When she was six years old she became a victim of this degrading torture. She underwent, as I did, the severest form of mutilation. As she tells her story I see these flashes: a dark room. She is naked and being held down. An old woman of perhaps seventy. She's wearing thick glasses. The cuts made again and again. 'My first question was Why? And my last question was Why? It is terribly painful and it isn't even anything to do with Islam!' says Bashra. She is quite distressed. I know how she is feeling. For me, too, images of the day of my own circumcision are flooding back again.

'Yes,' she nods. 'The memories are as clear today as they were twenty-nine years ago.' Bashra was on her sickbed for a full three months after the circumcision. For years she longed to have a chance to see the circumciser again. 'I wanted to kill her.'

She wanted to kill herself, too. 'When I had my first period, I seriously thought of doing away with myself.' I can imagine her sense of helplessness, her pain and her fear. 'There are things I can't tell you. I couldn't tell anyone, no matter how I try. It's like a film I have erased.

I often get nightmares; I can't bear to think about it.'
Bashra shudders, stands up and says: 'Do you know what
was one of the worst things for me, ever, Waris? When I
was a child I moved to Nigeria with my family and when I
was twenty I fell in love with the man I am married to now.
He comes from a part of Nigeria where FGM is not practised. The day before our wedding he took me to one
side. He told me that he had heard that Sudanese women
were circumcised and infibulated and he was praying that
it had not been done to me. It was one of the bitterest
moments of my life, having to tell him, 'Yes, it was done to
me, too. I am circumcised.'

Bashra's story affects me deeply. She lives in the middle
of Europe, isolated from her own family and her friends,
in a small suburban house near an English city. I can't
begin to imagine how many women are practically imprisoned in their houses and flats and never go out, because
they are stuck inside their own little world, not able to
communicate with others.

Bashra confirms my fears. 'Many African women here
have had no education. England is not their home. They
came here because of the political or economic situation
back home, not because they wanted to come here. They
dream all the time of being able to return and are afraid
they will be excluded from their society when they
return; afraid no one will accept them. You know that in
the Sudan uncircumcised women are thought of as
unclean. They are outcasts that people mock. This is
where we have to start educating them to realise that it is
a custom that is destructive and which must be consigned
to history.' Bashra speaks of her loneliness and her

depression. 'When I am in the Sudan and I have an argument with my husband, I can go to my mother or to his, and I can talk about what has happened, but here there's no one I can tell. I am all alone here,' she says, pouring out more tea. She found the birth of her first child particularly hard to cope with. 'When you are pregnant, you really need your mother, or an aunt, who can explain things and help you.'

When I hear these words I realise that there must be self-help groups which need to be put in touch with each other. FGM victims have to be able to meet together to talk to one another. How do we find these women? Most of them will be stuck indoors. There must be a way.

There are so many subjects that Bashra would like to discuss with someone whose experiences are similar to her own, for example, sexuality. 'I can't enjoy sleeping with a man. I never think about it, ever. Sex is something that just has to be done, a chore, something I just endure. Nothing more. I feel no arousal, nothing, nothing at all. How am I supposed to explain that? I love this man, but there's no sensation for me, none at all! It is nearly thirty years ago that they mutilated me. But when that part of me is touched it seems it was only yesterday I was cut. I can't get over this feeling, maybe the feeling is just in my head. Is there something really wrong inside me? Am I frigid?'

I can remember some of the messages posted on the internet site. Lots of girls are putting similar questions to these. 'Do you know you can exchange views on FGM with other women in the same situation, by going on the web?' I ask her.

She looks at me, amazed. 'What? I've been looking for an opportunity just like that. I didn't know.'

I think about Kadi and her desperate need to talk to someone who shared the same experience. We have to reach women with this information. That has to be one of the main aspects of our campaign.

'It has got to stop,' Bashra says suddenly. 'It just has to stop. If I and others here who are away from Africa just refuse to get our daughters circumcised . . .'

'But it is not just happening back in people's home countries,' I object. 'There are girls here in Europe, here in England, that are being circumcised.'

'Yes, I know,' says Bashra. 'Either they send the girls home to Africa or they ask a woman here to do it! Especially during the school holidays. I've heard from some other Somali women that there are professional circumcisers here in London. Other Africans do it, too – from Senegal. Or women from Benin or Togo, and from Mali and from Nigeria, too!' And then, after a short pause, she adds, 'And I know why they have it done. So the girl does not think about having sex with a boy. They want to stop you! That's why they do it!'

I think about these words later when I am back in my hotel room. How right she is! It does not matter what arguments are advanced in support of upholding this tradition. In the end it is all about power and control.

Next morning I phone Vienna. My researchers have got news for me. There's something coming up in Germany. We have heard about the clinics where genitally mutilated women are re-infibulated again after childbirth. More and more victims are contacting us and telling us how helpless the authorities are.

'I'm coming back tomorrow,' I tell my manager, Walter.

Most of the main efforts to prevent FGM in the UK are made by small, non-government organisations which have little in the way of funds and which have arisen directly out of the communities. These groups have been doing education work for over twenty years. They hold information evenings, they launch projects and do publicity; they circulate posters and leaflets. They also look after girls at risk and their families. But in comparison to the situation in France, their hands are tied. They are not allowed to visit schools, and social workers can only contact and talk to the teachers. There are no nationwide schemes to screen the girls by means of medical examinations at school or in health centres. All in all, the general level of awareness is so low that charges are hardly ever brought.

I will get together with the women from *Forward*, while Lea and Corinna will go to see the Black Women's Health and Family Support Organisation.

I have come across the name *Forward* countless times. Whenever I was talking to anyone in England about FGM, within moments someone would mention this group. It was the first, and is still the biggest, organisation of its kind combating FGM. *Forward* was set up in 1983 by the Ghanaian Efua Dorkenoo – first as a working party in the human rights group The Minority Rights Group – and then two years later they went independent. Anything done in the UK at all on the issue of FGM has an input from *Forward* in one way or another. That is not to say it is a large organisation with a few dozen workers and campaign offices. Far from it. *Forward* is small, very small. The annual budget in 2003 was £228,524 (330,672 Euros). The annual profits made by Manchester United would be enough to keep the group running for nearly forty years. Everything in life is relative.

The *Forward* office is in the Harrow Road in north-west London. This part of the city is well known for its ethnic diversity, but also for its poverty. It has the highest unemployment figures in comparison with other areas in the capital. Most of the people I pass in the street are from Africa or Asia. There is a huge range of different shops – Pakistani, Indian, African and Turkish. If you live here you are living in two different worlds: outside, it is England with its damp cold drizzle, inside – whether home, supermarket, bar or restaurant – it is the South. North-west London is home to half the world.

The office is on the top floor of an old factory which used to produce guns. It is like a warehouse or a New York loft, light, open and spacious. Here, too, paper clutters every surface and is piled on the shelves and the desks. Here, too, there are masses of files and a video library.

Adwoa Kwateng-Kluvitse welcomes me with a hug and a broad smile. She is the manager, the director, the press spokesperson, the lobbyist and the consultant, all in one person. She and her one assistant have everything in hand. We sit at the conference table and drink tea.

'So the FGM legislation alone doesn't solve everything?' I ask.

'No, you are right,' says Adwoa. 'First we fought to get the law to protect the children. In 1985 we had the

Female Circumcision Act making any sort of FGM illegal
in Britain. But a law is no use if it is not observed by the
community. Our first concern remains to educate people.
We train midwives, nurses, social workers and the police –
it is really important the police understand about it.
Police involvement is traumatic and FGM is a specialised
form of child abuse.'

'Tell me about the first law coming into force. Do we
know if it was effective in stopping circumcisions taking
place here in the UK?' I make my question very specific
because I want to be able to gauge the effect of the legislation that was passed.

'We know it is still happening in the ethnic communities, but that it is happening less often now,' is Adwoa's
answer.

'So they are still willing to have their daughters mutilated?'

'We only have research for individual communities.
The newest study was carried out in Birmingham,' says
Adwoa. 'But all the investigations point to the same overall result, namely that about a third of the people are
intending to have their girls mutilated.'

In Austria the figure is one third as well. One third are
clinging to the tradition – even though this destructive
and abusive ritual has been illegal for twenty years now.
Perhaps this is because no convictions have been
made . . . 'Were any cases of FGM uncovered here in the
UK?' I ask Adwoa.

'There have been two cases. In both cases it was a
doctor. In 1994 an Arabian doctor was caught by an
undercover worker. He lost his licence but was free to

practise again after three years . . . In 1999 an Indian doctor was filmed with a hidden camera conducting negotiations about doing the operation. He was going to do the operation at his own house, and he was asking fifty pounds for it. The video was shown on TV. Channel Four did a documentary about it – the film was called "Cutting the Rose". There was a tremendous scandal and the doctor was struck off.'

But the real scandal is that the doctors got away with it. They did not even have to go to court. The first one claimed he had misheard what the stooge was suggesting, and with the second one they could not have got a conviction because of the way the legal system works in England. You cannot have a murder charge unless there is a body and you cannot get a prosecution for genital mutilation unless you have someone prepared to come forward with a mutilated girl. 'And of course, we can't do that. We can't put a girl through that just so that the doctor can be sent to jail,' says Adwoa.

'Why do you think it is so difficult for mothers who have been living over here for years – and who thus haven't had to be confronted with the same social pressures as back home – why do they find it so hard to reject the practice of FGM out of hand?' I ask.

'FGM is such an emotive subject,' answers Adwoa. 'Women who have been through it have got an incredible psychological hurdle to get over. First of all they were violently abused and secondly, they were hurt by someone they trusted implicitly. That is the worst thing. If they have to admit it was wrong that is the same as saying "My mother didn't love me." That is very difficult. It is important to reach a stage where it is possible to say "my mother or my grandmother did this to me because they did not know any better. It injured me badly and hurt me and it was not right, but I still know that they loved me all the same."'

I know this dilemma all too well. I would never reproach my own mother with what she did. She did not know any better and she wanted to do the best thing for me. But I have admitted to myself that it was wrong. It was a long, painful journey for me too, especially because it is a subject nobody talks about. 'FGM remains a taboo. I am sure the communities did not take kindly to your broaching the issue.'

'Not at first, certainly not. They cursed us and insulted us; they pelted us with eggs and tomatoes. FGM is not something to be talked about. And because we did talk about it they said we had been "bought" by western culture, that we had "sold out". But it got easier with time.'

'You have been doing this work for over twenty years. In all that time something must have changed. You won't be able to reach them all, but some Somali families have been here since the fifties. How is it that after three generations the tradition is still so strong?' I still cannot get it into my head that there are still so many people who advocate the preservation of this terrible custom, although they should all know better.

Adwoa explains that it is because of the lack of proper integration. 'Look at how the Africans live here. They have poor housing and are crowded together. Many of them cannot read or write, especially the women, and they have little English. Even the immigrants who are

educated have problems assimilating. Their degrees or
professional qualifications are not recognised here in the
UK. And because of their refugee status they are not
allowed to work for a long time. This is very hard to take.
In a situation like that there is little incentive to adopt the
customs and values of the host country. On the contrary –
you hold fast to the traditions you brought with you from
home. These people have been uprooted and are completely isolated.'

'Would you say that is the case equally for men and
women?'

'Until now the women have been at a disadvantage
compared to the men. But now they are better off than
the men because it is easier for them to find work as
cleaners or maids, while their husbands can't get any work
at all and are dependent on their wives. They see everything collapsing around them and their reaction is to
become aggressive. They may mistreat their wives, but
also it makes them more likely to stress their role as head
of the family, so they insist on keeping up with the traditions in a way they probably would not have done if they
had stayed in their own country.'

'Hasn't a girl ever reported anyone?' I ask.

'No, they would never do that,' replies Adwoa.
'Children wouldn't want to get their parents sent to
prison. That would be unthinkable. And the parents
don't do it out of hatred for their daughters – it isn't the
same as someone beating a child or sexually abusing
them. The mothers want the best for their daughters and,
I repeat, they think they are doing the right thing for the
girl. Sometimes a girl will speak in confidence to another

adult, maybe an older sibling, or a teacher, because they are afraid their parents are thinking of getting them done. That is why *Forward* has set up a Child Protection project, and it is starting to work.'

So there is legislation on the issue but the law is constantly being flouted and no one is being brought to account. It is understandable that the children concerned do not make complaints. Even in France there has so far only been one such case. What is the role to be played by the organisations working directly with the communities? I am keen to see what Corinna and Lea have found out on the subject.

Lea, Corinna and I all meet up in a café in the middle of town. I give a short account of my visit to *Forward*. 'And what about the Black Women's Organisation? How are they dealing with the issue?' I ask them both.

Their response is not encouraging. 'Faduma Hassan is not a woman to mince her words,' Lea tells me. The Black Women's Health and Family Support Organisation was set up back in 1982, is the biggest organisation in the UK run for black women and was the first to take up the struggle against FGM. Their premises are in a back yard behind an unpromising-looking new building in the East End. 'At the moment the group's main aim is to publicise the new law as widely as possible.'

This is absurd, really. In March 2003 Parliament passed the law making it illegal for FGM to be inflicted on a girl even if the operation took place back in the country of origin. There was a media storm about it at the time. One year later the law was in force. But nothing else has

happened. The government did nothing to see that the
people affected by the new legislation were actually
informed about the change in the law. This would not
have had to be a huge publicity campaign because the
people involved are easily identifiable and can be targeted
directly. In the end it has been down to Faduma Hassan's
organisation to take on this task.

'They were given £20,000 in funding but that is just a
drop in the ocean,' reports Corinna. 'The group spent
the money getting posters printed, showing the main
points of the new law in all the community languages.
£20,000 is chicken feed.' She shows me one of the posters
printed in red in Somali: *Save the next generation! Stop the
mutilation! Keep out of prison!*

This kind of publicity campaign is sorely needed
because in many of the families concerned English is
hardly spoken and it is extremely unlikely that anyone
will be reading a newspaper.

'Why was so little money made available?' I ask.

The situation is actually worse still: there is not even
enough money in hand to enable Faduma Hassan, a specialist in this preventative campaigning, to work full time.
I cannot understand it. A law that nobody knows about is
going to be as good as having no law at all. Faduma's publicity material uses the threat of potential imprisonment
to deter families from clinging to the cruel custom. She
does not want to get anyone sent to jail – not even if they
are guilty of the offence. I ask my friends how Faduma
deals with a report of an intended mutilation.

The answer surprises me. 'The Black Women's
Organisation have a detailed plan in effect. If a social

worker hears about a genital mutilation being arranged, contact will be made with the Organisation first of all. Faduma goes round and talks to the parents. She stresses how important it is the police do not plough in there first and start arresting the parents. She thinks that would have a catastrophic effect on the family.'

How can the families concerned be convinced of the need to change their ideas? They need to be told that it is illegal and that the girl will be given a physical examination on her return to the UK.

'You can't go round arresting people who don't know they are doing anything illegal,' Faduma told Lea and Corinna. 'They think that an uncut girl will never find a husband – and in the eyes of an African mother that's the worst thing that could happen to a woman. They do what they think is the best thing for their daughters. We have to take that into account when we try to change things here.'

By the time we leave the café it is already dark and it has grown appreciably colder. All the same I take a walk through the East End. For centuries this has been the area where waves of new immigrants to the biggest city in Europe have made their start – looking for a fortune they seldom will have found. Ten thousand Somalis, that is a seventh of all those living in London as a whole, are crowded together here. Many arrived during the fifties, and then there was a second wave of refugees in the eighties, escaping from the war that is still raging in my native land. They live here in their own little world with no chance of getting work. Eighty percent of Somali men are unemployed.

I pass a small establishment where the curtains are pulled across the windows. There is a man on duty at the door. This is a Khat shop. Ninety percent of Somalis over here will take this African drug regularly. Khat is chewed. It is a bad drug, dulling your senses and at the same time making you aggressive. In Africa they would give khat to the boy soldiers. Somalis brought this habit over here with them, just as they brought the dreadful custom of genital mutilation.

Ninety-nine percent of Somali women have undergone the cruellest form of genital mutilation, namely infibulation. Unfortunately, many of their daughters born in the UK have been put through the same ordeal. Because the Somalis have been the target audience for most of the prevention campaigns, this has effected one change. Nowadays, instead of having their girls infibulated, Somali families are having the simpler, 'Sunna' method of genital mutilation carried out. However, the fact remains that the girls are still being mutilated. Is this all that can be done? No, I make up my mind, that is not all that can be done.

Of course I understand that the organisations working in the communities do not want to go in there like a bull in a china shop. Their aim is to be the interface between the main population and the immigrant families; they want to provide a useful link to the community, offering education, support and information. In a delicate situation where trust is paramount, it is counterproductive to crash in, calling on the courts and the police. They do extremely useful work and without these groups the immigrants would be unlikely to know anything at all about FGM being both harmful and illegal. The government does not seem to be spreading the word.

But the education programme on this issue should have been more or less complete by now. Attempts have been made for over twenty years to put an end to this cruel practice; the softly-softly approach has not had the desired effect and there has been little progress on this front. It appears that England is the destination of choice for African families from all over Europe when they decide to have their daughters circumcised.

Preventative work is essential, and forms the basis of concerted efforts. But in my opinion this is little use without the legislation actually being applied as a deterrent. The voluntary organisations on their own are not strong enough to get to the root of the problem.

4

'a child on its own cannot
protect itself'

In 2004 I was given the Social Award at the World Women's Awards in Hamburg. Mikhail Gorbachev presented me with my prize. I admire him for his work and achievements, just as I admire Nelson Mandela and the Dalai Lama. When there are big events like this awards ceremony, that are going to get a lot of media coverage, I like to use the opportunity to get as much publicity as possible for the anti-FGM cause. On that occasion I mentioned publicly for the first time that FGM was going on in Germany. At that stage I did not have exact figures or concrete data: my view was still based on hearsay about individual stories.

Our meeting today takes place in a small inn just outside Vienna. Corinna, Lea and Julia are seated round one of the tables at the back of the restaurant and papers and files are spread all over the table. 'Tell me what you know about Germany,' I prompt them. Paper rustles, files are opened and my researchers take it in turns to fill me in on the situation.

Germany is a tough nut. Nobody knows how many FGM victims are living there or how many young girls may be at risk. Twenty thousand? Forty? Sixty? The figures are vaguer than in the other European countries. According to the organisation Terre des Femmes, in 2003 there were fifty-six thousand-plus African women in the country who came from areas where FGM is the norm. As we know, fairly accurately, the percentage of women in the countries of origin who are circumcised, this should give a figure of approximately twenty-four thousand FGM victims in the Federal Republic. Roughly six thousand girls are at risk. So thirty thousand is probably the minimum number, given that, as in other European countries, there will be women who are living in the country without papers, and thus not included in the statistics. The anti-FGM activist Mariatu Rohde estimates that the number involved in Germany will double in the next ten years as immigration increases.

The actual number of victims is probably already higher than estimated. FGM is not only practised in the African countries, but also on the Arabian peninsula and in Asia, and these countries are not covered by the data. One of the voluntary organisations supporting women in Iraq, *Wadi*, carried out a survey in sixty Kurdish villages and found that sixty percent of the women there are genitally mutilated(!). Neither Iraq, nor Turkey nor Syria – all areas with Kurdish populations – have been studied with

regard to FGM. These results are of vital importance
when considering Germany because of the hundreds of
thousands of Kurdish people living there.

The legal situation in Germany is just as woolly as in
most of the other European states. This is scandalous.
There are two statutes – §224 and §226 of the German
Penal Code – covering the practice of FGM as dangerous
and actual bodily harm and assault. There is a potential
penalty of between six months and ten years' imprisonment, but no one in Germany has ever been charged with
having inflicted FGM on another. There are no specific
FGM laws. This means that clinics which carry out cosmetic plastic surgery can do procedures such as clitoris
reduction which would be illegal in Austria or the UK.
Furthermore, re-infibulation after childbirth is not explicitly outlawed. My researchers tell me that at the request of
her husband, a woman can be simply sewn up again after
the birth of a child – a demeaning and inhumane process.

The most serious problem, however, seems to be posed
by the FGM-Holiday syndrome, whereby immigrant families do not try to get their daughters circumcised in
Germany itself, but send the girl back to the land of
family origin. The practice is only illegal when the girl in
question is a German citizen. Unbelievable! As Germany
has one of the most restrictive policies as regards natural-
isation, the majority of the children of the second
generation do not have German nationality status. If the
girl goes home and is mutilated there, the person committing the offence gets away scot-free, together with
those involved in arranging the crime.

There is, however, a light on the horizon: In 2003 the

Youth Service in Dresden noticed that a woman from the Gambia was sending her five-year-old daughter back home to stay with the grandmother, so that the woman herself could go on a training course. The court that became involved withdrew custody rights from the woman and stopped the child leaving the country. The grounds given were that there was too great a danger of the girl being subjected to genital mutilation while abroad. This action of the courts, hopefully, sets a precedent. A High Court judgment in February 2005 has confirmed the decision. I breathe a sigh of relief. Germany is taking the welfare of the endangered girls to heart. They are ensuring that a girl is not allowed to be sent to a country where she would be at risk of the torture of mutilation. My optimism is short-lived. It is curbed by what I learn about Miriam.

Miriam is a young girl from Ghana. She is fourteen years old. She arrived in Germany three years ago after the death of her parents, when she had been supposed to be going to the home of her grandparents. Miriam is originally from the south of Ghana, where genital mutilation is frowned upon. However, her grandmother's second husband is one of the tribe elders in the district of Navrongo, in the north of the country. In this region the practice of circumcision is widespread, with an estimated seventy-seven percent of women affected. These figures are available in Germany and appear in a paper issued by the German Foreign Ministry in 2004.

Miriam's step-grandfather is a staunch advocate of the cruel ritual. This is why Miriam's grandmother decided to send the girl to Europe. On arrival, Miriam could hardly write and she spoke no German. Today she is one of the highest achievers in her school. 'I really want to be a doctor,' she says. But now she must fear for her future and indeed, for her life. Why?

Because Germany is on the point of sending this girl back to certain disaster. The asylum application is still being assessed but, at the beginning of February, the judge in charge of the case determined, according to reports in the newspapers, that the story lacked credibility and that the girl was not in danger.

Can it really be the case that in one and the same country there are such differing viewpoints being applied? One child is not allowed to leave the country, and in the other case a girl is to be sent away on her own? Luckily there are other people around, not just authorities. Many people in Hamburg were touched by Miriam's fate and they have formed an action group to support her. If Miriam's asylum application is turned down there are couples who have offered to give her a home and to adopt her. The people in Germany understand how vital it is to protect the girls, even if the authorities are slower to grasp the fact.

Germany is not at the top of the league in prevention work, either. On the one hand, groups like Terre des Femmes have been publicising the issue as well as possible for the past twenty years, but these organisations, which are working directly with African women from the refugee community and try to exert an influence for the good, are chronically short of money. The only official advice centre is in Frankfurt; the Berlin office had to close because of lack of funds. Government financial support had been cut.

I am horrified and surprised at the same time. Germany, the land of 'paragraphs' – laws to cover every living, breathing aspect of daily life – is turning a blind eye to FGM. I am clear about one thing: if we want our campaign to combat FGM in Europe to be successful, we are going to have to win here in Germany first.

I am in Berlin. Have I ever been here when it wasn't raining? There are said to be a hundred and ninety days of sunshine a year. What a shame I keep getting the days in between. We arrive at the first meeting, punctual to the minute. We are meeting Mariatu Rohde in a pizzeria in the west of the city. Mariatu has not arrived yet. She is an African who works as a doctor in the Brandenburg Clinic here in Berlin, and also runs the Afro-German network project called DAFNEP. We wait for an hour. We wait for another hour. Then we see a traditional German hat, a red one with a feather in it. Under the hat is a grand pile of dyed red hair. The hat and the hair belong to a black woman. She is wearing jeans and has a number of sparkling designer belts round her waist and she is carrying a huge bag. She sits down, placing her hat carefully on the snowy tablecloth. 'Isn't it great? I found it at a market,' she says, laughing. Not a word of apology, not a word of excuse about why she is late. But it is very difficult to be cross with her.

Mariatu cares little for the opinions of others and knows very well what she wants. She used to run the advice centre for FGM victims but now she is working full-time as a doctor, although she does the advice work in her spare time. She has set up her own website and does her utmost to campaign against FGM in her capacity as a private citizen and as a One Woman Band. She takes a pale yellow leaflet out of her bag to show us. Her new campaign is called 'Tell a Friend'.

'We are distributing these leaflets to girls in Neu-Kölln. That's the part of Berlin with the largest African population,' explains the activist-doctor. Weddings are the best time for handing out publicity material like this. Where else are you going to have such a great opportunity of meeting three or four hundred Africans all at once? 'If I hand out four to five hundred leaflets on one evening, this will bring in upwards of a hundred women in the following weeks.'

'How do you know which girls are likely to be at risk? It can't usually be sufficient just to check which country they are from,' I say.

'Of course not,' she says. 'I am from Sierra Leone, for example. The capital is Freetown. The people there are Creole and they do not circumcise their women. But in the hinterland the ritual is part of normal life for the whole population. These are the things it's vital to realise: you can't just generalise totally about a country and say that every woman from Gambia or Sierra Leone is circumcised.'

She is right! I remember some documents that I had read previously. According to UNICEF figures, around sixty percent of women and girls in Nigeria are affected. But there are two hundred and fifty ethnic groups in the country, all speaking different languages and all with their different attitudes and traditions concerning the special ceremonies and circumcision rites. Or in Yemen:

the World Health Organisation says that four percent of the women are circumcised – that country had never appeared in any of the statistics before!

Setting up an education programme in Germany about FGM requires great sensitivity. Mariatu has had many years of experience in this field; only an African woman can approach African women to discuss the topic. 'If a white person tells an African girl that FGM is wrong, she won't believe it. Even if she was born and bred here in Berlin. A subject like this can only be mentioned within the confines of the communities themselves – if at all.'

'Let's talk about FGM' was the slogan for a project she ran, inviting men and women to come along to a discussion evening. 'It was very lively. The men were quite prepared to talk about it – that's what was really surprising – they would never normally speak about an issue like that if African women were present. By the end of the evening even the oldest man there, and he must have been getting on for seventy-five, was standing up and speaking out against FGM.'

They ran another session to which only women were invited. 'One of the young women from Nigeria said the Europeans were always saying that circumcision took away your sexuality. This girl asked me how Europeans define sexuality. If I can't have an orgasm it is not always just the case that it's because of circumcision,' says Mariatu vehemently. 'Europeans like focusing totally on the concept of the woman's sexuality.'

Mariatu did not mean that white women should never get involved in discussions about FGM. 'African women appreciate their interest as long as they are sensitive about how they broach the subject. The more public airings of opinion on it, the better. But we won't have other people telling us how to handle our own culture,' says Mariatu, emphatically.

I recall the text I read on the homepage of Terre des Femmes, the largest NGO (non-governmental organisation) working on the issue of FGM: 'What we do in our campaigns lays us open to criticism that we are racist do-gooders interfering in the cultural affairs of others. We have managed to avoid reproaches of that nature because we hold that a woman's need for dignity and respect does not change from region to region. Human rights apply to all women, no matter where they live.'

'Right! And anyway, FGM is hardly to be equated with the concept of culture,' I say.

In order to prevent circumcisions being undertaken in the families' home countries, Mariatu has set up discussion groups with young girls and she offers a helpline for schoolgirls to use if they want to report a suspicion that a classmate is at risk. 'We have to reach the mothers through their daughters. It's particularly the German women, married to African men. They seem to embrace the customs in an overly submissive way, not feeling able to criticise African traditions, so they deliver their defenceless child into the hands of the family back home.'

Equally important in her eyes is the work they do to promote integration. 'I am constantly meeting women here in Berlin that have absolutely no contact with German society. Many of them have no papers. If they come up against the authorities they are not treated as people but as a problem that the Germans do not want to have to deal with. The women are often in miserably bad housing with no heating or water; the conditions will be cramped and hopelessly overcrowded. Physically we can say they are living in Berlin, but they hold fast to their traditions from back home – and with every good intention. They need to be introduced gently into the life here and given a chance.'

It is the same picture everywhere, whether in France, in the UK or in Germany. The vast majority of the African population in Europe live in isolation from the life of the host country. It is high time Europeans accorded these people the basis for a life fit for human beings. Integration is a matter of government policy and not of divine intervention.

I am surprised to learn that there is only the one advice centre for African women in the whole of Berlin. Berlin is, after all, a metropolis. The project was initially financed by the Senate Commission for Women and Health. Surely funding for something like that will not just be withdrawn? Here are two more stories to illustrate how important it is to have centres like this in Germany. Women affected by the practice of FGM are in real need of specialist help and advice.

For example, there was a man who left a distressed message on the answering machine at the organisation's office, his voice insistent and his speech disjointed with emotion. 'My name is Alex (not his real name). Please, please phone me back. It is urgent.'

When Mariatu returns his call he tells her, 'My neighbours are from Gambia. Their little girl goes to primary school here and now they are taking her back to Gambia on holiday. I have heard that female circumcision is often done in the Gambia, so I am worried that something will happen to her there.' But he would not tell Mariatu where he was calling from, what the family was called or where they lived because he did not want to cause trouble for them.

Without knowing the names, of course, it is not easy to help. But even if Alex had her told her the names there is little that Mariatu could have done. Germany is not as advanced as France in this respect. In France she would have been able to find out which girl was involved by means of a few phone calls, in spite of the initial lack of details. The network connections are much tighter over there. Once the girl had been identified, pressure could have been brought to bear, using the methods I described before.

In Germany there are practically no centres or official bodies or doctors specifically dealing with cases like this. The only thing that Mariatu could do was to encourage Alex to try and persuade the family himself not to take the girl with them. As he rang off he was sounding more hopeful. He did not call back again until a few weeks later – and the news was bad. What he had been afraid of had actually happened. The girl had been mutilated while she was in her parents' home country. A girl, born in Berlin, brought up in Berlin, but maimed according to African tradition. That is what reality looks like in Germany. It makes me furious, it makes me sad.

Take the story of Fatima (not her real name). The daughter of a Yemeni father and a German mother, she grew up like any other little girl in Berlin, attending kindergarten and then primary school. She had never been to the Yemen and only knew about it from what her family told her. Nobody had ever told her about FGM, of course. When she was eleven she was able to go with them when they went to the Yemen on holiday to stay with her grandparents. This visit would change her life. She was left in the care of her grandmother – and circumcised.

'Fatima was completely changed after that,' her school friends relate. Overnight she became very withdrawn; it was difficult to get a word out of her. Eventually she began to neglect herself and she started to put on weight. There were terrible rows with her parents and in the end she left to live in a children's home in Berlin. But her depression got worse and she was full of self-hate. At fifteen she made her first attempt at suicide. At sixteen she tried to jump out of a third-floor window. At seventeen she tried it again, only held back at the last moment by one of the staff. At last the truth emerged: the reason for her deep depression was the genital mutilation she had been sub- jected to. This abuse at the hands of people she loved, together with the knowledge that she was no longer like all the other girls – it had all become too much for Fatima.

The staff at the children's home did not feel able to cope with this either. They were used to dealing with the problems of children suffering violence or sexual abuse, but they had had no experience with the problems of a girl who had suffered physical and mental trauma of this kind. She was sent to a psychologist for treatment, but nowhere in Germany was there a single specialist for FGM that she could have been referred to. Nobody knows where Fatima is now.

'Only another African woman can help an African woman.' This I have heard time and again in Germany. Strangely, this does not seem to be the thinking in France. NGO groups in France report that lectures and events are attended by Africans and Europeans alike. I was really pleased to see that was the case. Since beginning to campaign on the issue of FGM I have often been confronted with the accusation that I am attacking my own culture – that I am betraying my own origins. I continue to insist that genital mutilation is not 'culture' – it is an abuse of human rights. An abuse of human rights that is committed against women the world over and which concerns all women the world over. We are not talking about traditional dances, ethnic food specialities or tribal customs. We are talking about torture of women. It is criminal violence against small girls. Every seventeen seconds somewhere in the world a girl is mutilated. This is a real problem demanding a real response: a loud and unequivocal NO! from every single one of us.

'We don't want people interfering in our culture.' This may be a slogan that many Africans believe in, but genital mutilation is not a suitable topic for arguing about who does or does not have the right to be campaigning for its total abolition. Every woman – no, every person – has to stand up against this cruelly misogynistic abuse. We all have to work together in solidarity in this fight for women's dignity.

On the subject of Africa there are many questions that
are still unanswered and that are crying out for attention:
centuries of oppression, hunger, the destructive rampages
of colonial powers, poverty, disease and lack of medical
provision. Africa is still being exploited by the rich industrial nations, so it is not surprising that Africans become
defensive when Europeans want to speak up on their
behalf. We can speak up for ourselves. Of course we can.

Germany has a number of excellent grass-roots pressure groups campaigning against the practice of FGM.
However, they are dependent on donations for their funding, and the amount of financial support they receive
from government sources is pitifully small. Charity fund-
raising is a hard-fought terrain. The enthusiasm and
commitment shown by these groups have managed to
make a start towards changing things. However, Germany
remains a developing country when it comes to preventative measures against FGM.

Nicola Egelhof is a sociologist working for DAFI, the
Afro-German women's group that is one of the classic
anti-FGM campaigning groups in Berlin. She is a slim,
energetic woman with shoulder-length hair. We go to see
her at her home, a romantic, ivy-covered house. It is a
lovely warm day and we sit out on the terrace. We are surrounded by amiable chaos: Nicola and her partner are in
the middle of doing up the house.

DAFI was founded in the year 2000. Now there are
only five people still working on what was initially planned
as a networking project. The idea was to set up a centre
for the two and a half thousand women in Berlin affected
by FGM. This led to the BAIP (the Berlin Project for

African Immigrants), the advice centre where Mariatu worked, too. 'When we were planning it, we wondered what the best format for a centre like this was. Going in to African families as a white German woman and telling them, "What you're doing is bad! You are harming your children!" – that's not going to get us anywhere. It has to be African women carrying the argument into these people's homes. They have to go out into the communities.' Some of the women who were originally involved in the group went on to set up their own support organisations. In Germany the pool of committed activists is easy to locate; it is a relatively small circle of people and everybody knows everybody else.

We start talking about FGM and the reasons behind the retention of this cruel ritual. Nicola Egelhof gets up, saying 'I wouldn't say that the idea of oppression is nonsense. The problem is much more complex. The mothers are using the practice to help their daughters integrate in their own societies, because that is the way it has always been done,' the sociologist explains. She has a great deal of experience of different African cultures, having travelled all over Africa working on projects funded by the Heinrich Böll Foundation. 'There is no point just regarding circumcision as an instrument of sexist oppression of women by men. I would argue vehemently against that view. In all the cultures where women are circumcised, men are circumcised, too. They take a piece of feminine nature away from the men and a piece of masculinity away from the women. An African belief has it that the clitoris is the penis and the foreskin is the labia.' She pauses. 'There are different takes on the subject. It's like this – depending on what society I live in, the circumcision of my daughter fulfils a different function: either to fit her for the marriage market, or as a rite of passage towards adulthood, or to protect her own health, to prevent her husband becoming impotent or to prevent her child becoming ill. These are practical functions. If we don't respect these attitudes we are not going to find the right way to tackle FGM and get it abolished. I also believe that it is not until women have access to education and independence that they will be in the position to stand up to these harmful traditions. This is what we should be concentrating on in order to target FGM effectively and to work towards eradicating it across the whole world.'

I have arranged to meet my research team for dinner. Julia has just arrived in Berlin. She has been to Hanau to meet Asili Barre-Dirie, who is a veterinary surgeon and who runs the German branch of *Forward*. Asili is very friendly and helpful. She comes from Somalia like me and she has the same surname as I do. For that reason the two of us are sometimes mistaken for each other. 'What are *Forward*'s activities here in Germany?' I ask Julia.

Julia takes a small cassette recorder out of her bag. 'Listen to what she told me!'

First Asili describes how she originally came across the topic of FGM in Germany: 'In 1994 I was trying to save a little girl from being circumcised. I talked to her family and managed to persuade them not to have the operation done. I did that without going to any organisation for advice. It made me want to do more to help.'

She heard about Terre des Femmes and got in touch with them. They asked her along to a meeting. 'When I got there I saw about thirty or forty women and they were all white. I was the only one who looked different. We talked about FGM and I said, "We have to go out and speak to the African women." They all turned to look at me in surprise. "Oh, we can't do that," they said. "No, you can't," I said. "But I can!"'

In 1999 she got together with some other women and established *Forward Germany* and has been working in the organisation ever since. One of their projects was putting on an exhibition of Nigerian art on the subject of genital mutilation. She has set up many lectures and discussion evenings in the communities, not to put victims on show but to talk to them about their experiences. *Forward* also organises weekend seminars for girls of 'African background'. Asili keeps emphasising the importance of approaching the women and girls with the utmost sensitivity, whether trying to explain to circumcised girls that they are still full and complete as women in spite of the operation, or persuading mothers not to have their daughters circumcised. Asili enjoys the contact with other groups: 'But there are always slight differences in perspective. I always try to approach the women concerned directly. I call it my "grass roots" work. Of course I have a much better chance of gaining access to the women properly than any of the German activists do. I can understand what they are telling me. A German woman would not be able to understand.'

Asili describes a convention of the various help groups, who meet together on an annual basis. 'I know we have got to improve communication between the groups. We will be so much stronger if we can work together on this. We have to try to get a network in place in Germany.'

Julia forwards the tape: 'In Europe people have only started to discuss FGM since the publication of Waris Dirie's books. There are lots of groups committed to help the cause. Some of them are to be taken seriously and some of them are a less positive influence, generalising dangerously and speaking in harmful clichés and saying stuff like, "Look at these barbarians and what they do to their own children." Or they point at an African woman in the street and tell people, "That woman over there will have been circumcised." I've even known it happen that there's a discussion on the topic in class and the teacher turns to one of the black girls and asks her, "Have you been mutilated, too?"'

I think of Kadi again and hope nothing like that ever happens to her. All teachers, medical staff and social workers must receive proper training in how to deal with the subject of FGM when addressing victims. This must be an important aspect of my campaign.

Julia is about to switch the cassette player off when I catch a sentence that goes right through me. 'Hang on – can you play that bit back again?' I ask her.

You can hear a pin drop as we listen again intently. Asili says, 'Our children have the same rights as German children. The same right to be protected. As long as they are living here. A child on its own cannot protect itself.'

That is the heart of it. I think of all the girls I have had contact with: Kadi in Paris, Tabea in Vienna, Bashra in

London, the girls on the Internet forum. And I think of myself as a child. I think of little Waris.

A child on its own cannot protect itself. The phrase echoes round our heads all evening.

I have been asked to do an interview with a journalist from a German newspaper. I arrange to meet her in the Twelve Apostles, a well-known restaurant in the Charlottenburg district. I've got that apprehensive feeling again in the pit of my stomach. It is the same paradoxical situation over and over again. Here I am, a world-renowned model, but in most people's eyes I am first and foremost the victim of a barbaric tradition. I have given countless interviews in my lifetime. Most of them centre on the topic of FGM. That is the way it should be, given that I am campaigning to have the cruel practice abolished worldwide.

As I step into the restaurant a young woman with short blond hair waves to me. We order coffee and then she starts the interview, 'Ms Dirie, can you describe how you came to be victim of this dreadful ritual. How did you feel at the time?'

I look at her in horror and sense that my apprehension is rapidly turning into anger. 'What did I write my books for? I put myself in front of you all, in front of the whole world, and I said "Look what happened to me". But I did not do all that to satisfy any voyeuristic tendencies people may have. I did it to help children who are under threat of the same treatment. And to get FGM stopped.'

The young woman looks shocked. She apologises. Next

question: 'How do you feel today? Do you have a fulfilling sex life?'

Enough is enough. I am not answering questions like these. I stand up, turn round and leave.

Why are Europeans so insensitive and so lacking in respect? What they really want is for me to break down in tears. Then they could show the picture round the world: the helpless woman. The victim of a barbaric ritual. Pity her! I need their pity just about as much as I need appointments with politicians who only want to pose for a photo with me. Arm in arm. 'United in the fight against genital mutilation,' they could have as a caption. And they would do nothing. I have done enough posing for photographs in my life. The subject of FGM is too important to me for me to allow it to be cheapened with publicity stunts like that. I decide to go for a jog in the Berliner Tiergarten park to calm myself down a bit.

The next morning Berlin's air is clear as glass and it is a splendid autumn day. I jump straight out of bed and inside half an hour I am ready and out. I have agreed to take part in an anti-colonial Africa conference. The weather is too good to waste it in a taxi so I set off for Berlin-Kreuzberg on foot with a hundred thoughts whizzing round in my head.

Why is there so little respect for African women in Europe? Why are we so often seen as fair game? Why is an African woman seen as a 'native' even if she is from a cultured, educated and prosperous family of high social standing?

This image of the African woman owes a great deal to the European attitudes that emerged in the colonial period. Everybody knows that Britain and France had vast colonies. But Germany had colonies in Africa as well. Back in 1884 the continent of my birth was divided up between the great powers of Europe at the Berlin Africa Conference. They divided it up using a ruler. Germany got Togo, Cameroon and Namibia. The native populations rebelled against the colonial power as their countries' riches were transported back to Europe and both land and people were ruthlessly exploited. The uprising was brutally quashed and the war of suppression continued, culminating in the wilful massacre of nearly all the Herero people.

Hardly anyone in Berlin knows about the horrors perpetrated in Africa under German colonialism. Nobody took the subject up when it was drawn to their attention. For over a hundred years the Herero have been clamouring for compensation for the genocide. They have had no success. They are still demanding the return of bones and skulls from thousands of their people, stolen by German scientists engaged on research in eugenics. These body parts are still stored in Germany and have yet to be returned.

To mark the centenary of the massacre, some members of the Herero tribe are here in Berlin to attend the conference I am going to. As well as publicising the centenary they will be wanting to raise awareness of Germany's still largely unchanged attitude towards Africa. As part of the fringe programme for the conference there is to be an 'anti-colonial tour' of the African quarter of Berlin.

We meet up in front of the Springer building. Opposite the glass palace the conference is taking place in the courtyard behind one of the houses. There are workshops and lectures to go to – but everyone who can get a place has come along on the trip. The bus is full of students, Africans in traditional robes, university professors and Human Rights activists.

We get out when we reach the Togostrasse: a street like hundreds of others in Berlin. It is just the name that is unusual. We are told the history of the city district in three languages: German, English and French. We learn that there are twenty-three street names around here that remind Germany of its colonial past. For example: Togostraße, Kamaruner Straße, Otawistraße, Lüderitzstraße and so on. The Bremen merchant Lüderitz financed the first fraudulent purchase of land that formed the core of what was to become known as German South West Africa. Nachtigalplatz is a square named after the Kaiser's special envoy, Gustav Hermann Nachtigal, who forced through the 'Protectorate treaties' for Togo and Cameroon by employing a mixture of deception and gunboat diplomacy.

We are speechless. How can Germany still be honouring these men in the street names of the capital? But there is worse to come: The name, African Quarter ('Afrikanisches Viertel'), our guide tells us, goes back to the original plans of the famous zoo-owner from Hamburg, Carl Hagenbeck. He was putting on exhibitions of people from other lands. These shows were very popular at the time – one huge colonial exhibition in 1896 in Berlin had a hundred Africans on display. Encouraged by this fantastic success, Hagenbeck planned to create a desert landscape specially designed for a

corner of the park in the 'Rehberge', where, alongside
African animals, African people would be on display,
living there permanently. The First World War put an end
to these plans but the name remained.

So – African men and women were put on display to
entertain the Berlin populace! You could stare at them or
feed them peanuts. The Germans who visited the exhibitions of this type would not have been plagued by scruples
because they would have regarded the Africans as hardly
human. My ancestors, in cages.

During the Nazi era German imperialist colonial aspi-
rations grew. The Petersallee was named in honour of
Carl Peters, celebrated by the Nazis for his renowned
activities in the colonies. He had forced through treaties
under threat of military might and thus provided the
foundation stone for the German colonies in East Africa.
He was known to be sadistic in his treatment of Africans;
he bore the nickname 'Hänge-Peters' (String-'em-up
Peters). People he did not like the look of, he had
hanged, quite simply. Our guide told us about another
development in this part of the city: in 1939 the allot-
ment area was named Togo and the name hangs over the
entrance to the gardens even today: 'Permanent colony
Togo.' How can that be allowed, we wonder. 'It had nothing to do with colonialism,' says a passer-by, irritated by
our reaction. '"Kolonie" just means settlement, so it
means permanent settlement.' That would be the typical
instinct of the man in the street, to avert his gaze and not
think about the deeper significance.

Not only the man in the street, but also the city
authorities have problems dealing with this legacy,

explains the guide. 'As early as 1946 attempts were made to have some of the streets renamed but none of the changes were accepted. Again in the eighties people tried to get a new name for the Petersallee. There was a choice of various African celebrities from past and present, like Samuel Maherero or Nelson Mandela. There was so much argument about it in the city parliament that in the end they decided to leave it as it was, as Petersallee, but they found another Peters it could be named after. So now it is Hans Peters, a relatively unknown local politician, not Carl, the Colonial.'

Is anyone here proud of that particular idea?

The health service in Germany is not adapted to the needs of women who have been subjected to genital mutilation. It was only a year ago that the topic of FGM was introduced on training programmes for doctors; the same is true of the situation in Austria. In spite of these attempts to improve things, there are still a large number of doctors and nurses who know nothing about the subject. They certainly do not know how to deal with patients who are affected by FGM. Women are having to face humiliating attitudes and degrading treatment in hospitals and consulting rooms. Perhaps a doctor has diagnosed a mutilation and then calls in a colleague to show them 'what this sort of thing looks like'. There is no code of conduct governing medical staff on this issue, and only a few seem to grant the patients the tactful approach they deserve and so desperately need. I think of Kadi and how frightened she was of doctors. No wonder, the way they sometimes treat us.

Here in Berlin there is one specialist doctor for two

and a half thousand FGM victims. Lea and Julia met her while we were on our city tour. Sabine Müller is a gynae-cologist working in a family planning clinic. The advice centre, Balance, is located on the second floor of a Berlin shopping centre and offers information, medical treat-ment, and advice about pregnancy, contraception, sexuality and relationships. Treatment and advice are free, whether or not a woman has health insurance cover. At last. I am delighted to hear it. Finally we have people here who see the person first, giving the paperwork sec-ondary importance.

When Lea and Julia visit the clinic there are three women and a young couple in the waiting room. The atmosphere is subdued and the secretary is very busy. She announces, 'The journalists are here, doctor,' briefly over the intercom. It is obvious she thinks there are more important things on the agenda today than giving interviews.

Half an hour later Sabine Müller comes in. Her manner is somewhat distant at first. Her short brown hair is tousled. She takes Lea and Julia into one of the other rooms. Sabine lights up a cigarette and tells my researchers about the first time she came across the phe-nomenon of genital mutilation: 'It was back in the eighties and the magazine *Emma* had just published an article about it. I was a medical student at the time and I had no idea at all that there were women who looked completely different down there. Nobody had bothered to tell us that when we were studying human anatomy, of course.'

Ten years ago she was confronted with her first case of FGM. 'It was a woman from Ethiopia and she was circumcised and infibulated. When her husband left to go to Germany he had her re-infibulated so that he could be sure she would stay faithful while he was away. Some time later he fetched her over to Germany to join him. They came to my surgery and asked me to reopen the scar as they wanted to have a second child. She had already given birth to one baby by Caesarean section because nobody had the courage to attempt the opening of the infibulation to allow her to give birth naturally.'

'Were you prepared for dealing with their request?' asks Lea.

'I still remembered what I had read in that *Emma* article, years before, and there had been illustrations to make it clearer,' answers Sabine, 'so I wasn't exactly shocked by it. Particularly because the woman was treating it as if it were perfectly normal – for her it *was* normal.'

'What is your approach when dealing with a mutilated woman?' asks Julia.

'You need to be just as sensitive in dealing with a victim of FGM as you would always try to be in dealing with a victim of rape – very cautious and tactful. You have to take care not to say anything like, "Oh my God, that looks awful".'

A woman once told me that she had had the worst question in her life put to her by a doctor when he had looked between her legs. He said, 'For heaven's sake, have you had a car crash or something?' It made her feel totally humiliated. Harry Gordon, the doctor in the Well Woman Clinic in London and one of the best-known FGM experts in Europe, makes a point of ensuring that staff are aware that such insensitive comments have no place in the consulting room. 'Nobody working here would get away with showing disrespect by derogatory remarks or disparaging gestures on sight of a patient's mutilations,' Harry told me.

But unfortunately this happens all too often. A survey in Canada showed that eighty-three percent of those interviewed felt that they had not been treated with enough respect when they had to attend hospital appointments. Forty-seven percent of doctors had reacted to FGM patients with indignation and disgust.

It makes me think of Kadi again. And of the story that Ishraga told me. Of the doctor who called his colleague in 'to have a look at this'. I am furious. It is essential that all the professionals who are likely to come into contact with these women are fully aware of the importance of reacting with sensitivity.

Back to the visit to Sabine Müller. Julia asks her, 'What can be done here to help women who are circumcised?'

'About twenty percent of my patients have the most severe form of FGM, infibulation. We offer a small operation to open up the barrier of tissue; it is called de-infibulation. An opening is made and if enough material is extant, a reconstruction of the genital area can be attempted. I keep the extent of the operation to an absolute minimum to avoid traumatising the patient.'

'Does that involve a reconstruction of the clitoris?' is Julia's next question.

'If the clitoris has been removed, then it is not possible to replace it,' replies the gynaecologist. 'What is gone is gone. But often the clitoris can be found under the bridge of scar tissue and we can attempt to expose it again.'

A great deal of time is spent with the women in preparatory talks before the operation takes place. 'The women need to have explained to them that their urination will be affected and that the stream will be much stronger than what they are now used to,' says the doctor. 'It's vital to explore with them the probable changes they must expect, because a strong stream of urine when they pass water is considered in many of the cultures that practise circumcision and infibulation to be vulgar and uncivilised. When they use a public toilet after the operation has increased the opening, they know that other women will be able to hear them passing water. They have to learn not to be embarrassed by that and also to come to terms with what their vagina will look like. Many women are proud of being circumcised as they feel it makes them clean and they do not have any obvious outward genital characteristics, only a smooth skin barrier.'

'Would you encourage such women to undergo the opening operation?' Lea wants to know.

'We are very cautious about that. We only do the operation when a woman is very keen to have it done and has been properly prepared for it emotionally. Sometimes it might be two or three years before she gets to that stage of readiness. Most of the women just come to get information; they want to know why sex is difficult, what is the matter with them. Then again, many of them are happy to leave things as they are.'

'Do you try and include the men in the decision-making about whether or not the operation should be done?' Lea asks.

'Of course, absolutely. The women who have the operation here and have coped successfully with the change it
brings will be the ones who have discussed it thoroughly
with their husbands first. As a rule the men are happy
with the result. It is terrible for the man if the woman is
always in tears when they have sex because of the pain she
is experiencing. Men want to be loved and desired and
they want their women to enjoy the act and to look forward to it.'

'Have you had patients who have requested re-
infibulation?' asks Julia.

'No, and I would refuse to do it,' says the doctor.

'Sometimes re-infibulations are carried out in German
hospitals following childbirth. What do you think about
that?' asks Lea.

'That is a different situation. If a woman who has been
circumcised and infibulated turns up as an emergency in
the labour ward and has to be cut open so that the baby
doesn't suffocate, then it would be your duty to sew the
woman up again afterwards. She has a right to that. She is
likely to lose a lot of blood if the cut is made during
labour because the whole pelvic area is flooded with blood
during childbirth. For that reason alone, if for no other,
you would have to see that the woman is sewn up properly,
at least provisionally. I repeat: I think she has a right to be
sewn up again. Emergency surgery is not the same as a
decision taken over time and involving the views of both
partners. Put yourself in the following position: imagine
that you, as a European woman on holiday in Africa, were
to go into labour early. You give birth and the doctor sews
you up afterwards. You would take the hospital to court

about it, wouldn't you? You would go all the way to the highest court in the land to settle the case. Perhaps you can start to realise now what it would be like for an African to feel that some self-important doctor had just decreed, "What you've got here, it shouldn't be like that at all – we're going to cut it open and afterwards it is to stay open, whatever you may say",' explains Sabine to illustrate her point of view.

I think of Bashra in London. She told me that after the birth of her first daughter she had been sewn up again. It was the norm then in England to do that. Today, thank goodness, it is not permitted.

I wonder what goes through the head of a doctor when he carries out a re-infibulation. The original state of the woman would be the body before she comes in to the hospital. Now that is not the case when a woman has been mutilated. Lea tells me what she heard in conversation with someone from the Society of German Midwives: 'I came across that in Germany once. This husband wanted us to sew his wife up again straightaway. So we did. Just not so tight as before. A bit less, so that at least she could pass water properly . . .'

I feel anger rising in me again. Is anyone in this country thinking about the women? How is it this man can decide that his wife should be sewn up again, that she should be infibulated for a second time? Perhaps he will come back and demand it a third or a fourth time. I have heard all the arguments. Of course, the woman has asked the hospital to put everything back, after she gives birth, to the way it was before. So, sew up the opening! Has anyone thought about why she wants that? Why should any woman request that she is restored to a state that is demonstrably bad for her health? Because she knows no better? Or because she does not really feel she has a choice in the matter?

My meeting with Comfort Momoh comes back into my mind. Did she not say that women hardly bleed at all when the infibulation is opened up, but that repeated slicing of the scarred area with subsequent re-stitching is very harmful for the condition of the tissue? A doctor is a professional, an expert. Is he not obliged by his Hippocratic oath to improve my health where it is possible to do so? I cannot understand this attitude. Perhaps the error lies elsewhere. Perhaps we need to ensure that the doctor does not have this conflict of interests. It is certainly better when there is clear legislation on the subject as is the case in the UK. A doctor who is asked to perform re-infibulation would then have to refuse, saying, 'No, it is against the law.'

Back to Sabine Müller again. Every year she sees roughly a hundred women for treatment who have suffered genital mutilation. The youngest patient was seventeen, the oldest was fifty. 'Do you talk to your patients about their intentions on circumcision for their daughters?' Lea asks her.

'Yes, of course,' the doctor answers. 'You have to believe in what you are doing and do your best to put the message across. If they are reluctant to discuss it I let it go, but I certainly ask them all if they would be intending to get their own girls cut – any woman that comes to us in the first place has been thinking about the issue for some time. We have other patients where it's already too late to change anything – their daughters have been done already. I had a few women in my care who were wanting to go ahead with the procedure for their girls because they were giving in to family pressure. All I can do is to try and persuade them not to do it. If they feel they don't have the strength to stand up to their family, I suggest they just pretend to go along with it. She could arrange for the cutter-woman to visit but then just kill a chicken, splash the blood about a bit and then tell all the neighbours that it's done.'

'And if that doesn't work?' asks Julia.

'Then I am powerless to do more.'

'You wouldn't report it to the authorities?'

'If I did, I would be sure of losing any influence I have and any trust the women of the community have placed in me. And that is the last thing I want.'

'Do you know about genital mutilations that take place here in Germany?' This is Lea's next question.

'They wouldn't tell me about it, of course. But I have heard rumours amongst my African acquaintances that lead me to think that the rate is about fifty/fifty – with about half of those families intending to get their daughters cut by sending them back to Africa on holiday for the procedure, while the other half will try and find medical intervention here.'

There we have it again. I should not really be so affected by the revelation any more, but I am still shocked to hear it. That genital mutilations are carried out in all the European cities I am visiting makes me feel that the rug is being pulled out from under my feet. Again and again in London, Paris, Amsterdam, Berlin: people on the ground working with the ethnic communities in these places are all aware that FGM is carried out right there under their noses. In spite of that, apart from in France, there has not been a single prosecution of either a doctor or a circumciser. In practically all of these countries either journalists or pressure groups have attempted to track down doctors who are doing these illegal operations. Why are we not getting any cases to court?

But, evidently there are doctors prepared to re-infibulate a woman after childbirth at her husband's request. What happens here when a mother asks a doctor to mutilate her young daughter? I pray that the answer would be that no doctor would agree to do it and that they would alert the authorities or, at the very least, they would try to persuade the mother to change her mind and not have her daughter mutilated in this way.

5

they do it here, too

Doctors, male or female, play a vital role in the situation with FGM. Often they will be the only ones who get to hear of the woman's problems, so it is crucial that they are well informed on the topic and that they have the ability to deal sensitively with the women they treat. They can prevent impending mutilations by being aware of the possibility and by alerting the authorities when they suspect offences are being committed. By reporting their suspicions they can ensure that other children in the same family are kept safe from the danger of mutilation and do not become the next victims. But do the doctors actually do this?

We want to investigate this and are looking for an African woman who can contact some doctors for us. After a few days we find the right person: Flora (not her

real name) is from Nigeria and has been living in Austria
for a year as an asylum seeker. She is dead set on doing
what she can to combat the practice of FGM: 'It is a hor-
rific crime.'

We go through thoroughly with Flora what she can
expect when she visits the doctors for us. She will introduce herself as Theresa Okafor from Nigeria and she will
ask for an appointment for a circumcision procedure for
her (imaginary) daughter Beatrice, a seventeen-year-old
about to get married – to a Nigerian man. She will give
this as the reason why the operation is being requested.
We get to work with a list of gynaecologists and paediatri-
cians, concentrating for simplicity's sake only on doctors
practising in Vienna.

Flora starts working through her list, using the speak-
erphone so that we can hear both sides of the
conversations. The first few calls are no good. The recep-
tionists do not speak enough English* to be able to
understand what the appointment will be for. Or else they
refuse to put 'Theresa' through to speak to the doctor –
she would have to come to the surgery to talk to him. A
few of the doctors evidently do not understand what it is
about and keep asking what is the matter with the daughter, what her symptoms are.

Finally we get the first result: a longer exchange with a
doctor. He has a foreign-sounding name.

'Good morning, doctor. My name is Theresa Okafor. I
have a problem and I hope you can help me. I am from
Nigeria and I have a daughter. She is seventeen.'

*All the calls are conducted in English.

'Seventeen?'

'Yes, seventeen. I want to get her circumcised. I need a professional doctor to do it.'

'What is wrong with your daughter?' the doctor enquires. He has a very deep voice and he speaks English with a strong accent.

'Circumcision. I want to get her circumcised. Can you do this procedure?'

'Right, circumcision.' A pause. 'Stay on the line. I will see when I have time.' After a short pause he says,' I will have to speak to my colleague. Give me your number and I will ring back.'

A few minutes later Flora's mobile rings. It is the same doctor again. His manner is abrupt: 'Come here tomorrow. Six p.m.'

'How much money shall I bring?'

'Two hundred,' says the doctor. 'Bring two hundred euros.' Then he rings off.

The next evening at five-thirty p.m. we set off for the doctor's surgery, which is on a main road in a typical Vienna council-housing block from the fifties. Flora goes in and tells the doctor she wants to discuss the details of the operation with him. The doctor seems surprised. He says he had misunderstood on the phone the previous day. He had thought she had been talking about a boy needing circumcision. Now, is he going to threaten to report her to the police? Or will he attempt to get her to drop her plans and change her mind?

No, neither of these options. The doctor apologises. 'I am sorry, but I cannot do that,' he explains to Flora. 'It is illegal; there is a prison term of six months on that. I can't do that.'

Flora acts the innocent and tells him back home where she is from circumcision is normal practice. The doctor is sympathetic and tells her, 'Yes, I know it is the custom in Sudan and other countries in Africa but you will have to have it done over there. We are not allowed to do it here.'

A little small talk follows. Flora says she will keep looking, and off she goes.

In the meantime, we have been waiting in the car outside. As she recounts what happened we are amazed. Not a word of criticism of her request. On the contrary, the doctor actually advised her to travel back home to get the operation done. What next!

In France if that had happened the doctor would have been under obligation to report it and social workers, police and doctors would have gone into action.

In the evening we go over the conversation again. We wonder if it was really the case that the doctor has misheard in the first instance. We have the nasty suspicion that he had understood quite correctly and wanted to assess the situation – in principle he did not object to the idea of carrying out a mutilation.

A week later we get back to our telephoning. We soon have the next appointment. Again, the doctor has a foreign-sounding name. Again, Flora puts her enquiry: 'Doctor, I have a problem. I need a circumcision for my daughter.'

Again she is given a prompt appointment. She is to come the following day at five o'clock. We accompany her to one of Vienna's prosperous districts. Only the doctor and his receptionist are still at the surgery when we arrive. The doctor speaks broken English. Flora has to repeat her request several times.

'Ah, you want a circumcision for your daughter. The genitals.'

'Yes, circumcision.'

Only now does the doctor realise what is required. He says, 'It is very difficult here in Vienna.'

Then the receptionist joins in, 'Isn't it banned, anyway?'

The doctor responds, 'It is not forbidden but it isn't really permitted. It can be done privately. We'll have to see what we can do.' He pauses, then continues: 'I don't do it myself, but I know someone, another doctor.' He turns to the receptionist and tells her, 'Find me Dr H.'s number.'

Then he turns back to Flora. 'Doing the operation in Austria is a problem. They don't like it here. They say it is not good for women. They think it is an African tradition. I have had women from Angola here who wanted to get it done. I referred them on as well.'

Again the receptionist objects, 'But isn't it illegal?'

A short, dismissive reply, 'Oh, if you only don't take much away, it's OK. Give her the number.'

Flora takes the piece of paper, thanks him and goes.

Again. The doctor is not horrified at the request. He makes no attempt to get her to re-think her plan. This is a gynaecologist in Vienna and he gives her the address of a colleague straightaway, and it is not the first time he has dealt with a similar referral.

The next day Flora phones Dr. H. She explains what she wants. 'My daughter is getting married. I want to get her circumcised, the traditional way.'

The doctor hesitates. Then he says, 'I can't discuss this on the phone. You will have to come here. Give me a phone number where I can reach you.' His tone is sharp.

Flora gives him her mobile number. He soon rings back. An appointment is arranged.

'Come round now with your daughter,' he instructs.

'How much money shall I bring?' asks Eleonore quickly.

'I am not discussing that on the phone,' she is told. The doctor rings off.

Flora conducts a few more telephone enquiries, with much more promising results. 'That is illegal! Tell me your name, so that I can report you!' thunders a renowned plastic surgeon. I doubt this reaction would have put anyone off and changed their mind if it had been a genuine enquiry, but at least he was indignant.

Flora turns up at our Dr H.'s surgery, in a council block in one of the poorer districts of Vienna, taking a 'daughter' with her – a nineteen-year-old Nigerian girl who could still pass for seventeen. Inside the consulting room the girl has to stand; only Flora gets offered a seat. 'I want to have my daughter circumcised,' Flora opens the conversation.

'Is that what she wants?' the doctor asks when he has understood what the 'mother' is asking.

'Yes,' says Flora, 'It's because she will be getting married.'

Without wasting a glance at the 'daughter', the doctor

asks, 'Who is the husband? Why does she want this done? Is she still a virgin?' And finally he turns them down . . . 'We don't do that. It is not right.' But instead of trying to persuade Flora to abandon her plan, he advises her: 'You will have to go to a clinic. She will need an anaesthetic. She can't have a circumcision without anaesthetic.' He notes down the name of a well-known Vienna hospital and gives her the piece of paper. 'Try there. They may be able to do it for you there.'

This is where we break off the experiment. We have heard enough: hardly a single gynaecologist in the whole of the capital reacted appropriately to our fictitious request. Some apparently thought it was legitimate to circumcise a girl who was still a minor. The three doctors Flora went to see at least would not have carried out the procedure themselves – but they were prepared to refer her on.

Our research shows that the practice of FGM has only recently become the subject of disapproval among European doctors. In the middle of the nineteenth century the Viennese gynaecologist Gustav Braun was praising the technique of clitoris removal as a female cure-all. He published a paper in the capital's medical periodical, *Wiener medizinischen Wochenschrift* under the title of 'Amputation of the clitoris and the inner labia as a treatment for vaginismus'. He describes the case history of a twenty-five-year-old who suffered from convulsions after receiving a head injury in a fall. His diagnosis was vaginistic attack, a cramping of the vaginal wall muscles. He cauterised the external genitalia. As recovery did not

ensue, he went on to remove the clitoris and the inner
labia. After a hospital stay of six weeks, the patient was
sent home, considered cured.

About a year later Braun published an article entitled:
'Further discussion on the treatment of masturbation by
means of amputation of the clitoris and the inner labia.'
Here he reports on a twenty-four-year-old woman 'of good
family' who had been masturbating since her fifteenth
year. The clitoris and the inner labia were removed with
the consent of the patient and the patient's mother. In
hospital, a nurse noted that the patient was 'fingering
herself under the bedclothes'. The fingers were band-
aged individually and then the hands wrapped in a towel.
As the patient made no further attempt to satisfy herself
she was considered to be cured and was released from
hospital.

We do not, thank heavens, have any Gustav Brauns in
Europe anymore. However, European doctors are not
doing what they can to help eradicate FGM. This has to
change as soon as possible. Every doctor must be educated about the subject and every doctor must act
responsibly in this area of medical provision.

While looking for doctors who are prepared to carry out
FGM in Europe, I have come across a new concept,
namely *the designer vagina*. 'Go to London,' I was told.
'That's where the most expensive private clinics for cosmetic surgery are to be found. They will do a designer
vagina for anyone who can afford to pay for it.'

Of course I went to London to investigate. It is easy to
find private clinics for plastic surgery there. The clinics all

have posters showing the perfect female body for us to admire, and the text explains all the things a woman can do to her body, from botox injections to chin and cheek re-modelling, face-lifts, breast augmentation, liposuction, wrinkle removal and nose-jobs.

It makes me shudder. In my time as a model I saw my fair share of the mania for cosmetic procedures and plastic surgery. I still find it perverse to see what European women are prepared to do in the name of beauty. Nobody forces them to do it: it is their choice. It is abominable that they do not even stop when they reach their genitals. Among the procedures on offer are reduction of the labia and of the clitoris. If these operations are on offer, we must assume that there is a demand for them.

Sabine Müller, the German gynaecologist and FGM specialist, wrote about this phenomenon in an article for the human rights organisation known as Terre des Femmes. 'We have seen cosmetic surgery done on breasts, thighs and hips. Now it is the turn of the genitals to be transformed with surgery, tattoos and piercings: up to fifty piercings on one person's genitals. Amongst my patients I have more and more German women who chose to have the hood of the clitoris removed. They have noticed that they have purchased the heightened pleasure sensations at the cost of hypersensitivity and a painfully dried-out organ. And this is not all. Patients are always asking me how they can have their inner labia "tidied up" and reduced. These women have become victims of a beauty craze that trivialises the genitalia – a craze that is subtly permeating our whole society.'

The Internet is full of webpages on aspects of cosmetic
genital surgery. A quick surf-through shows that this is
not just a UK issue, but one that is rife in Germany as well.
Dozens of clinics offer labial and clitoral reductions and
remodelling of the pubic mound. All of this undeniably
falls under the World Health Organisation definition of
female genital mutilation and is thus illegal in the UK.
Nobody seems to be bothered by this.

I find it difficult to believe and I study the Internet
sites more closely. It is becoming more and more absurd.
There is a list of available operations that makes me think
of a catalogue of spare parts for a car. You can re-tune and
streamline your genital area just like you can tune an
engine, it seems. Here is one entry: 'If the inner labia are
too large they may hang down, looking unaesthetic. This
can be very distressing for the woman. Long labia can get
in the way during certain activities, for example, cycling,
and cause discomfort, or they may rub and become sore
if tight trousers are worn. They may cause embarrassment
and the woman may not like to show herself naked, which
will have a detrimental effect on her sex life.'

Particular techniques are advertised as being suitable
for this condition. A laser is the preferred instrument as
causing less blood loss and being more precise in application. Exact measurements are taken in advance of the
amount of tissue to be removed, in order to achieve a
symmetrical result. The superfluous flaps of tissue are
removed and the wound sewn with tiny stitches which will
later dissolve by themselves. 'There are also cases where
the outer labia are underdeveloped. Here it would be
possible to augment them with padding tissue taken from

the patient's own body – fat from the abdomen, for example, can be specially prepared for re-insertion in the genital area. It is not necessary to make incisions of any real size.'

Or again, another offer from the menu: '*clitoris*: particularly because of hormonal insufficiency during the embryonic developmental stage the clitoris may be affected in size and appearance. These abnormalities can be of a variety of types. The most common is an oversized clitoris. On reduction it is vital to preserve blood supply and sensation. The clitoris must be retracted under the skin by the relevant amount. A circumcision of the clitoris entails removal of the hood (Praeputium clitoridis). The clitoris itself remains untouched. It is exposed by this operation. It retains all of its sensitivity.'

Or '*pubic mound*: the most common operation in this area is the correction of an overly prominent pubic mound. It is reduced in size by suctioning off some of the excess fatty tissue. In a few cases it may be necessary to tighten the skin to some degree.'

I go on reading, to be told what motivates women to agree to procedures such as these, to actively desire mutilations of this order. 'An estimated twenty-five percent of women in Germany suffer from "unaesthetic variations" in the genital area, whether these are congenital or acquired,' a German doctor writes on his website.

'Going to the sauna, to a naturist beach or even just undressing in front of other people can be torture, with relationship difficulties and emotional problems becoming inevitable,' warns another doctor in Germany. He adds, 'Correction to the labia minora should not be seen in isolation: they form an aesthetic whole with the hood of the clitoris and the outer labia. For this reason it is quite usual to restructure the whole area and tighten the tissue up to give an attractive and harmonious overall result.'

Only one surgeon attaches a warning clause: 'As with any other surgical procedure there is always a possible risk of infection, swelling and discomfort.'

In the Internet forums where women can describe their personal experiences with operations of this nature you read about worse things than that: loss of sensation, numbness, loss of libido and loss of pleasure, swelling and intense pain. I come across the following stories of suffering posted on the web by young women:

Flower:
The inner labia are still a bit longer than the outer ones. I find that rubs against my underwear and it inflames the scars. I wanted to know if you find the same thing with the inner lips still protruding. Did it heal up eventually and stop hurting?
Witch:
I only had the op on Monday. Everything still very swollen and painful.
Flower:
After the op I couldn't sit for days – I had to keep lying down. I thought the pain was going to kill me. It is true: long labia are NOT ugly, but I checked that out too late . . . I wish I hadn't had it done.
Jenny:
I had the laser operation under general anaesthetic, but another doctor said he would only do that

operation using a scalpel, rather than laser, because there are no advantages and there is the risk of burns. It looks like all the doctors have different views.

Joy:

I had it done three months ago. It doesn't hurt. But the inner lips swell up a lot sometimes when I have sex and that can hurt. I never had that before the operation.

Witch:

Question to all of you: Has anyone had the stitches burst? The right-hand side has come open and it looks pretty gross. Don't know if it'll heal up by itself or if I will have to go back to the doc? I've changed my mind about the whole thing. I'm not half so keen on it now.

Joy:

It cost me 1020 euros. It was really worth it for me because I don't feel I've got to hide my pussy all the time. If you're having it done, get them to use laser or electro-excision, otherwise it bleeds a lot. And it has to be tightly stitched – there can be problems.

Martina:

I'm from Luxemburg and I had it done in a beauty clinic in Brussels – I got the address off the Internet. At the moment I'm not happy about it at all. It was done five days ago and it still hurts and it's all swollen. It's so swollen that I can't see if it even produced the right results. I'm really getting worried, reading in the forum about all the other botched operations.

African women are mutilated, European women choose to put themselves under the knife. Here, where so many will shake their heads in disgust at the thought of our barbaric practices, women get surgical procedures done in pursuit of beauty. Here, where they point at us, the victims of FGM. Here, where we are exhibited as exotic creatures on display. Here, where they call us backward and barbaric: in this oh-so-civilised Europe, FGM is practised in dozens, in hundreds of clinics, quite officially. Not only that. Women are deceived into thinking that an 'average' genital region is in fact 'ugly' and 'not normal'.

Of course, we can't compare this to what happens to women in Africa, where they are subjected to FGM. There, it is mostly defenceless children who are violated in a terrible ordeal. Here we are dealing with adult women. Over there, many of the victims are forced to have the vulva sewn up. Here, we are only talking about reduction in the size of the inner labia and the clitoris. Over there the clitoris is often cut out altogether. Over here, the clitoris is 'only' exposed, 'reduced' in size, made more 'aesthetically pleasing', even if often with dramatic consequences.

But still, over here or over there: Flesh is still being cut and the woman is still the victim. Even when she is choosing to make herself the sacrificial lamb.

In the West there is evidently a specific beauty ideal for the genital region, and this ideal image is not so very different from the African one. The woman is to be made to look as far as possible like a young girl. People are obviously afraid of anything that is clearly a sign of a mature woman. Her sexuality must be constrained and controlled.

When we talk about Africa, people say it is the men who demand it, even if it is the women who carry it out. What about here in Europe? Here as well, women want to conform to some idealised version – presumably a male ideal – of what is considered beautiful. Who else are these designer vaginas being designed for?

I am still in a state of shock. How could anyone in their wildest dreams think it is a good idea to snip and slice away at their genitals in pursuit of beauty? I am amazed. Quite apart from the common sense aspect, is it even legal to operate on a vagina to prettify it?

In the UK it is not. In Austria it is not, either. Any oper-ations that could impair a woman's ability to experience sexual sensation are forbidden by law, even when the woman requests the procedure. Where is the dividing line?

I ask someone who ought to know. Edwin Turkov is a surgeon and university professor in Vienna and he also runs a cosmetic surgery clinic where labia minora cor-rection procedures are carried out. 'Where is the dividing line between correction procedures and FGM?' I ask him directly.

His opinion is clear: 'The one case involves the labia being corrected if they are too big and are causing dis-tress, and the other case involves the clitoris – that is the dividing line. The clitoris must not be touched.'

'But there are doctors in Germany offering operations to reduce the size of the clitoris?'

'I will say it as starkly as it deserves to be said. Anyone altering the clitoris is committing a crime.'

The people running German cosmetic surgery clinics do not see the issue quite so clearly. A few phone calls were enough to demonstrate that there is no difficulty trying to find someone who will do a clitoral reduction operation, or remove the clitoral hood or lower the clitoris. With the appropriate financial resources and a measure of discretion it is possible to find someone prepared to carry out work of this kind on a young woman. Is there perhaps a further, hidden meaning behind a slogan like, 'Whoever can afford it will have cosmetic surgery'?

We phone Dr X, one of a dozen people specialising in this field.

'Good morning, Doctor, my name is Maria Berger. You were recommended to me for operations in the genital area. I have heard that you do clitoris reductions.'

Dr X: 'Yes, we do many of these operations here. The procedure is quite routine – we have a lot of experience with it.'

'May I speak freely, Doctor?'

Dr X: 'Of course.'

'I am to be married soon, to a man from Morocco. In his country it is the custom to have quite radical clitoral reductions. I would like to get a result that is close to that idea.'

Dr X: 'You want the clitoris not to be visible?'

'Can that be done? To have it not visible?'

'Yes, it can be done. The hood of the clitoris is removed and the clitoris itself is lowered so that it can't be seen.'

'And the inner labia are cut away at the same time?'

'Not necessarily, but this can be done at the same time.'

'You will be familiar with the Sunna technique of circumcision. That is what I want done.'

'That technique entails mutilation. The clitoris is actually excised, cut away.'

'Yes, that's what I mean. Do you do that?'

'Ms Berger, you must be clear about this. What is gone, is gone. It can't be repaired afterwards. From a surgical point of view it is quite straightforward and is actually a simpler procedure. But is that really what you want?'

'Yes, I've had a good think about it.'

'Well, it's certainly possible. But you should go away and think about it some more. It involves a mutilation, after all, and I would have to consider whether it is ethical.'

'Maybe you know of a colleague who could do it?'

'No, no. Just come back to me about it in a little while. I will have to give the matter some thought. My function as a doctor is to make people more attractive.'

'But surely it is a cultural issue, whether or not a certain thing is considered physically attractive?'

'You have a point.'

'You see, the thing is, I don't want to have it done over there. I'd rather have it seen to here in Germany, with a specialist doing it.'

'I tell you what – just give me a little time to think it over. I have to go to my consulting rooms now. Let's make an appointment.'

'So you could do it?'

'We'll have to discuss it in person. You will have to have thought about it carefully.'

'What would it cost?'

'Reducing the labia costs two thousand euros, and lowering the clitoris costs a further thousand. The rest we would have to talk about.'

Several other phone enquiries produce similar results. Most of the cosmetic surgeons are easily persuaded to contemplate the treatment we suggest and are prepared to cut the clitoris on payment of the relevant amount. They react helplessly if objections are made about reluctance to accept the beauty ideals from other cultures.

Here is an extract from a phone conversation with a doctor who initially refused to do the operation:

'You do surgery on breasts, cutting them and filling them with plastic. Where I come from that's seen as a barbaric thing to do – a woman's breast is intended to give life.'

Doctor: 'Yes, but lots of women are distressed by having breasts that are too small. We help them. That is something else.'

'But you could help me, too. I live in a country where it is considered beautiful to have a smooth genital area. It is not your function to decide what is or is not beautiful, just to help a woman attain her own ideal of beauty.'

'Yes, you're right, of course. Perceptions of beauty are different from culture to culture.'

'Where do you draw the line? What is the difference for you between reducing the size of the labia and removing the clitoris?'

'Well, medically, it's not a problem. But you would have to live with having no sexual sensations any more.'

'But that would be my own decision.'

'Yes, you are right. Why don't you come and see me and we can talk about it.'

In Austria it would be illegal. In Germany you just have to find a few hundred euros to get the clitoris circumcision carried out. 'You would have thought,' writes Sabine Müller, 'that humans would have learnt over the thousands of years to leave the genitalia as they find them. Sadly, this has never been the case. Organs designed by nature to give sensations of pleasure have been subject over time to a variety of tortures and there is no end in sight to this attitude.'

No end yet in sight. Particularly not for Arab and African girls. The shocking thing is that evidence points to an increase in genital mutilation in Europe. 'It is done here too. We know it is.' No matter which of the European countries I have visited recently, I keep hearing the same thing.

The question of where and by whom these terrible operations are carried out is hard to answer. There are three possibilities, really: in a doctor's surgery, in cosmetic surgery clinics, or with the help of the traditional circumciser. But everyone carrying out the procedure in Europe knows very well it is against the law.

People tell me about lists of names and telephone numbers that are passed around in the communities themselves, giving details of the circumcisers. Anybody working to eliminate FGM like myself will not get access to a list of that kind. In addition, there is the phenomenon of 'circumcision tourism'. Girls are sent right across Europe because there are places you can get it done more easily or more cheaply, such as Amsterdam and, especially, in Sheffield in England. These are the current 'hotspots' in Europe.

Reporters all over Europe have gone undercover in dozens of cases to expose the occurrence of genital mutilation. In Britain the newspapers found two doctors – both of them still in practice today. German TV broadcast a documentary on the current affairs programme 'Monitor', filming a doctor undertaking negotiations about a circumcision. However, the victim was not in a position to go to court and so the case was dropped. I have already cited the case in Austria involving undercover work for the journal *profil 2001*. The doctor in that case, too, is still practising.

While in Europe it is mostly doctors performing these procedures, in Africa it is usually female circumcisers. They hold an important position in society with this function and they make good money for themselves from their appalling occupation. I have heard of circumcisers being offered payment and alternative work if they will agree to give up their trade. What a terrible idea! Millions of women in Africa are without enough food, let alone an income. Why on earth should the circumcisers be rewarded for giving up their evil trade? These women have been responsible for the deaths of countless young girls. In my homeland a third of young girls will die as a result of the procedure, either from loss of blood or infection contracted at the operation. Victims who survive all say the same thing: they are able to forgive their own mothers but they will never forgive the woman who circumcised them – they would rather kill her.

These women are actively carrying out circumcisions in Europe as well, as we know from the case in Cardiff, but only three cases have led to the conviction of a circumciser. The most recent was in France in 1999, and the reason the prosecution was successful in that case was that, for the first time ever, a victim reported a circumciser to the police. The young woman, from a Mali family, was twenty-three at the time. She had been mutilated by the woman previously, but when she heard that her younger sister had been subjected to the same thing, she went to the authorities. From then on the circumciser was under surveillance for weeks and her phone line was tapped. Finally the police got the tips they needed, but it took another five years to collect sufficient incriminating evidence to secure a conviction. The trial ended with the woman being sent to prison for eight years on a total of forty-eight counts.

A few days ago I heard from a social worker in Germany that some Nigerian families were planning to get a midwife to come and circumcise their daughters. At my insistence, she gave me the number for Pastor Anthony (not his real name), the Nigerian priest who had given her the information. I got into contact with him straightaway. He spoke English with a typically Nigerian accent. I quickly told him the reason for my call, but he would not give me any details because of being bound by the confidentiality of the confessional. 'You must understand,' he told me, 'I am a priest – I can't just pass on information. The community trust me. I cannot and will not risk sacrificing that trust.'

When I go on to ask him if there is any truth in the rumour I had heard, he does at least admit the following: 'I can confirm that there are plans in the community for carrying out a circumcision. I cannot tell you any details.'

Shortly after that my phone rings and there is an African woman on the line. She sounds nervous and distressed: 'Some families here are getting together to have a circumciser come and do their daughters. She'll be coming over from Holland in the next few weeks and she will do the circumcision mutilations on several girls.' She does not know – or she does not want to tell us – any of the details.

The same thing all over: it does not matter where we make enquiries, we soon hit a wall of silence. There are always the hints, usually very similar ones, but no access to concrete evidence. It is enough to drive you crazy. Lots of people know. Nobody says.

6

it has nothing to do with religion

I dream about a girl. She is five, or perhaps six, years old.
She is black as the night, with wild hair and huge eyes.
She is lying on an iron bedstead covered with a green
sheet. The room she lies in is dark, cold and empty.

The girl is afraid. She is quivering with fear but staying
still otherwise. Only now do I realise why. She is tied down
with heavy dark brown leather belts at her wrists and
ankles. Her legs are spread wide.

The door opens. Five women come in. She cannot see
their faces. Nobody speaks.

One of the women is carrying a white kidney-shaped
dish. In it there is a razor blade. The other women have
white cloths. The circumciser stands at the foot of the
bed in the middle of the room. The women group round
her. Nobody says a word.

The circumciser kneels down in front of the girl's spread legs, puts her little dish on the bed and takes the razor blade in her right hand. Then she moves her hand towards the girl's genital area.

Suddenly the room is flooded with a stream of light from above. A voice rings out: 'Don't do it. Stop! It is against our religion.'

Then it turns deathly quiet again. The light has disappeared. The circumciser lays the razor blade back in the dish. She stands up and slowly leaves the room. The women follow her in silence.

The leather constraints have gone. The girl sits up and finds herself in the middle of a flower-filled meadow. Kneeling next to her is the girl's mother, saying, 'It is over. It is over for good.'

Who do people listen to most? Their spiritual leaders, I am convinced of it. Genital mutilation would disappear overnight if the leaders of the world's religions were to say, 'Mutilation is contrary to the ethical principles of our religious community. Stop doing it.' No law, no education programme, no police intervention, no prison sentence and no political campaign could ever be as effective as a religious leader taking a stand. With only those five words – 'it is against our religion' – they could end this horror.

A vision? Perhaps it is only a vision now. I hope it will not stay that way for ever.

I was raised as a Muslim. I believe and I pray. In spite of that I am not steering Boeings into skyscrapers. I do not strap explosives to my body and get on to crowded buses. I do not try to kill anyone who does not share my belief.

In times like these it is necessary to state this quite clearly: the majority of Muslims in Europe and worldwide are peace-loving and despise violence just as I do. A number of militant rabble-rousers are doing their best to destroy what is the common aim of thousands of tolerant people in Europe: to make it possible to have people of different cultures, skin colours and religions living side by side in peaceful co-operation.

Violence rules the world today. Today mosques are burning. The good ship 'Europe' is in danger of foundering. What will go overboard? And where are we heading ?

November 2nd, 2004 in Amsterdam was a day like any other. The thermometer struggled to maintain decent autumn temperatures. Around nine o'clock a big, middle-aged, fair-haired man was cycling along on the canal side. In the Linneaustraat another rider came up behind him. When the two men were about level with each other, the second man pulled a gun and fired six shots. The victim attempted to escape and fell off. The assailant hurled himself on to the fair-haired man, drew a knife and cut his throat. Then he skewered a five-page confession on the knife and stuck it into the man's chest. A bus driver using her mobile phone camera managed to get a photo of the dead man. The picture went around the world.

The assassin with his long beard and his *djallabah* remained standing triumphantly beside the body for a few minutes before running off. He was arrested half an hour later after shots were exchanged with police. He was a Dutch citizen from a Moroccan family, twenty-six years old and a member of the Islamic terrorist scene in the Netherlands.

The victim: Theo van Gogh, forty-seven – the painter was his great-great uncle. Theo van Gogh was a film director, agitator, *enfant terrible*. He produced nineteen low budget films (six of them funded out of his own pocket). He had a reputation as one of the strongest critics of Islamic fundamentalism, and he had harsh and coarse words for radical Muslims: 'a horde of mediaeval goat-fuckers'. He had commented publicly that he intended to emigrate because 'Holland was turning into a kind of Belfast with burning churches and burning mosques'.

Another thing he had said: 'I will be murdered on the streets.' He uttered these words a year before he was killed.

That day in November 2004 Van Gogh had been on his way to his office to put the finishing touches to his documentary *06/05*, about the politician Pim Fortuyn who had been murdered 911 days previously. It was the day the Netherlands, that celebrated paradise of liberal attitudes, was to lose its innocence. 'Flames in the land of multi-culturalism' – these were the world headlines. Eleven minutes were enough to turn the country on its head.

Eleven minutes – the length of the film, *Submission, Part I* that Theo van Gogh directed, which was shown as part of the culture programme on the VPRO channel of Dutch television. It was about the subjugation of women in Islamic society. The film was made in English with Dutch subtitles. In it, four young Islamic women, portrayed by actresses, described how they had been married off by their fathers, enslaved by their husbands and mistreated, raped and made pregnant by an uncle. The images are forceful. The women kneel in a house of prayer, dressed only in light transparent chadors, their faces veiled except for the eyes. Bellies, legs and arms are covered with phrases from the sura of the Koran and with bloody marks from lashes. A short scene in which a badly beaten woman is pouring out her heart to God is flashed into the film repeatedly. In the background a beating can be heard taking place.

'Oh, Allah, Almighty One, you tell us that man is the protector and owner of woman because you have given him more strength,' prays the woman. 'At least once a week I feel the strength of my husband against my face. Oh Allah, Almighty One, life with my husband is so hard to bear, but I bow to your will (. . .) I feel trapped like an animal waiting to be slaughtered.'

The script for this short film is by a Somali Muslim woman, Ayaan Hirsi Ali, who lives in Holland. She is an energetic politician who fights strenuously for the emancipation of Islamic women, particularly for their liberation from the cultural shackles of genital mutilation.

Ayaan Hirsi Ali is in her mid-thirties. She was born in Mogadishu. Her mother was the fourth wife of a Somali politician who brought his daughters up strictly according to the tenets of Islam. For political reasons the family had to leave Somalia, landing up first in Saudi Arabia and then in Kenya. When Ayaan Hirsi Ali was a teenager she was married against her will to a nephew. She was expected to spend the rest of her life as a housewife and mother. She escaped from the 'prison' and with the help of friends travelled through Europe, eventually settling in the Netherlands. She understood

not a word of Dutch at first, and worked as a cleaner
and then in a post-room. When she had mastered the
language sufficiently she studied Politics at university,
supporting herself at the same time by working in
women's refuges and in abortion clinics. It was then
that she broke with Islam. Today she speaks of the
prophet Mohammed as a 'tyrant' and of Islam as a
'backward culture'. After she graduated she became
active within the social democrat political party PvdA,
changing to the right-wing liberal VVD before the election in 2003 and has been a member of the Dutch
parliament since then.

November 2nd 2004 radically changed her life. The
five-page tract found on the body contained a death
threat directed at her. 'I know that your end is near! I
know, unbelievers, that for all of you the end is near.'

What struggle is being fought out here? A battle of cultures? A war of religions? A fight against genital
mutilation and for the emancipation of women?

The Netherlands has been seen for decades as the
model country when it comes to tolerance. What is not
expressly forbidden is permitted. A third of the Dutch
population is of 'non-western origin', with Islam here
the most widespread of the religions. Most immigrants
live in isolation, in their own communities in
Amsterdam, the Hague or Rotterdam. Seventy-five percent of the immigrants will marry within the circle of
their compatriots. Sociologists speak of the so-called 'parallel worlds'. In the other big European cities the
situation is not much different.

If you talk to the women in the foreign quarters of

these cities you will soon notice that they are not living in a parallel world but on a different planet. 'Hardly anybody in Holland is as isolated from society as Muslim women,' confirms Ayaan Hirsi Ali. 'It is like being in a cage.'

My Somali sister is fighting for a new anti-FGM law similar to the current legislation in France. She is demanding that girls from risk areas are given an annual physical examination from birth to the age of eighteen; furthermore, the legislation would involve legal proceedings against parents and circumcisers alike, should a mutilation have taken place. Also, people known to have assisted in operations of this kind will be registered in a central database. They would be banned in the countries of the European Union. The current legal situation in the Netherlands is that anyone who arranges genital mutilation for their daughter in Senegal or the Sudan will get away scot-free because these practices are not banned in those countries.

There are about thirty-nine thousand women in Holland who have come from 'risk states'. Most of them arrived in the eighties or nineties from Somalia. No one knows how many girls and women in the Netherlands have been subjected to FGM. 'It could be ten women a year, or it could be a hundred every year,' says Anke van der Kwaak, the Dutch anthropologist and FGM researcher.

A new law? There were soon enough people lining up to register their objections. It would be inhuman and racist to pick up a particular group of girls from specific countries and subject them to physical examinations, they claimed. The Netherlands debates the issue hotly while thousands of girls are still being mutilated every year.

I am no Koran expert. My experiences, my education and my instincts determine my lifestyle and my attitudes, as for so many other people. I reject violence, polygamy, subordination of women and genital mutilation, because deep within me I feel that all these things are wrong. It is not a view I came to as a result of my investigations and research. Religion for me is not only the scripture: it is what we as human beings make of the Holy writing. It does not matter whether we are Christians, Muslims or Jews.

Because I am trying to find out why many people who advocate FGM base their arguments on the Koran while, on the other side, so many say that the practice is not mentioned in the Koran with a single word, I arrange to see Amina Baghajati.

Amina was born in Germany. She came to learn about Islam through her husband, and she converted after 'mature reflection'. She lives in Vienna and chairs the Austrian Human Rights organisation, SOS Mitmensch (fellow human being); she is the mother of four children and devotes herself 'with great love' to studying the Koran.

When she opens the door to her house I do not recognise her at first. I have never seen this slim woman with the long black plait without her headscarf before. Her children are romping about in the living-room. Amina brings me tea and we swap items of personal news.

Then we get down to the main issue. 'We are starting

to discuss FGM in our religious community, but the taboo has to be broken down with great sensitivity,' Amina tells me.

'What is Islam's position on FGM?' I ask her quite directly.

'The Islamic position is quite clear,' she answers. 'There is consensus that FGM should not be practised. FGM is a crime against women.'

'Then why is Islam so often connected in people's thoughts with FGM?'

'Because many of the countries that defend the practice mistakenly base their arguments on Islam. But there is no mention of the practice in the whole of the Koran, and certainly no recommendation of it. FGM as a phenomenon pre-dates Islam.'

'Does the Koran not also stipulate the need to respect the physical integrity of women?'

'Yes. The body is seen as a gift from God. This is why cosmetic operations are not permitted. Moreover, in Islam the woman has the right to her sex life. If a woman is not given sexual satisfaction in her marriage this is seen as grounds for a woman to sue for divorce. Islam is not hostile to sexual pleasure. A fulfilling sex life within a marriage is considered a good deed. The use of contraception is permitted in Islam. The most crucial point for me is that the prophet Mohammed, whom all Muslims try to emulate, did not have his own daughters circumcised.'

I tell Amina my plan to set up an education programme to publicise the issue of FGM. She greets the news warmly and stresses how important she feels it is to inform and enlighten those affected. 'It is vital not to spread the word in any way that could be interpreted as interfering European paternalism.' She goes on to tell me about an incident that impressed her. 'A young man asked his fiancée during the time of their engagement whether she was circumcised. When he heard that his future wife was "alright", i.e. that she was circumcised, this news was not alright for him. He broke off the engagement even though he got on well with the girl. He said he would only contemplate marrying an uncircumcised woman, a woman whose genitals were intact, so that marital relations would be without health problems and pain. This brings home to us that it is the women each time that are the victims of the publicity about this inhuman tradition – the same women who were the victims of the original circumcision. All the same, education to increase public awareness of how harmful and destructive FGM is will not of itself get the practice eradicated.'

In the evening I watch a documentary about two Turkish women. One of them is blonde, cheerful, and smartly dressed in the western style. The other is brunette, wears a drab dress and headscarf and her speech and facial expression seem to mirror a life that has been full of disappointments. You would not realise that they are the same age, thirty-two, unless you listened carefully to the commentary. Judging from their appearance alone, you would put a good ten years between them.

We are shown how the trendy blonde girl buys material – she works as a designer – how she meets her friends in the evenings and dances and laughs. The brown-haired

Turkish woman, shown in her simple home, drinks tea
and worries. At the end of the report comes the surprise:
the blonde does not live in Paris or Berlin but in Istanbul,
the brown-haired woman lives hidden away in the middle
of Germany since her family cast her out because she is
divorced. The only connection between the women is that
they are both Turkish, and both Muslims.

The next day at the office I tell the others about the
film. They all smile. 'Seriously,' I sum up, 'that's what
makes it so difficult to talk about FGM and Islam. Because
there is no one single such thing as "Islam".'

Corinna objects, 'You can't claim that Islam and FGM
are not connected at all.'

'Yes and no,' I reply. 'We can't just cut off the discussion in mid-air and bring it all down to the simple
formula: FGM is Islam's fault.'

'But how is it that genital mutilation is mainly found in
Muslim countries?' asks Julia.

'Well, that's true,' I say, 'but we have to consider one
thing: the structure of Islam is quite different from
Christianity. In Islam there is no figure like the Pope who
hands out all the moral decisions about the way his flock
should conduct themselves in life. In Islam there are different schools: conservative, modern, fundamentalist or
progressive. Each school of thought interprets the Koran
in its own way. So I can't just say: "Here is Islam and it is
responsible for FGM."'

'But you have to admit that the religious leaders in
Islam seem to be pretending that genital mutilation is
not a problem,' says Lea. 'And it's not just them: women
are an inferior class in all the religions – in Christianity,

Woman is held to be responsible for the Fall, and for the fact that Man was thrown out of the Garden of Eden. And I haven't heard a lot of Imams making pronouncements condemning the practice of FGM.'

'That is not quite right. FGM is being discussed more and more – and there are very lively debates on the issue. The thing is that what we hear about is what the trouble-makers are shouting about.'

We talk some more and then I pull a handful of leaflets out of my bag. 'Look at these,' I say. 'I've collected them for you. These are things you need to know about Islam.'

I get my things together and get ready to go home. It has grown dark and cold. I put my hands in my coat pockets. Of course I mean what I just said to the others in the office about Islam and FGM. It is not the fault of the Koran if FGM is being mostly practised in Muslim countries. But religion bears the responsibility.

In Europe little is known about Islam. This religious community is the second largest after Christianity. Over a billion people – nineteen percent of the world's population – are practising Muslims. Within the EU they have been a significant group for a long time. In France about six million people belong to this faith – about ten percent of the entire population; in Germany there are over three million, in Britain two million, and in Austria there are three hundred and forty thousand living according to the tenets of the Koran. In Germany alone the number of Muslims has doubled in the last twenty years.

Islam is a monotheistic religion: in Islam there is one god, Allah. His revelations were written down in the

Koran, a collection of more than six thousand verses –
there are no stories here as there are in the Bible, but alle-
gories, vows and praise, offering a great deal of room for
interpretation. Every Muslim is bound by five doctrines,
the five pillars: he believes in the one god, Allah, he
believes in Mohammed as Allah's prophet, he prays five
times a day, he pays alms ('Zakat', the equivalent of two
and a half percent of his yearly income), he fasts during
Ramadan, and he makes a pilgrimage to Mecca.

Islam permits a man four wives, but only on condition
that he treats them equally well. Sex within marriage is
seen as being pleasing in the sight of God, while outside
marriage it is forbidden. Before Allah, men and women are
equal. On earth, however, the woman must obey the man.

The founder of the religion is the Prophet
Mohammed. He was born in Mecca in the year 570. Allah
appeared to Mohammed in nocturnal visions in the form
of the Angel Gabriel many times over a period of twenty
years. As the Prophet was unable to read or write he dic-
tated an account of his visions to his scribes. Directly
following Mohammed's death in the year 632 the writ-
ings were collected, revised and grouped into a hundred
and fourteen chapters, the Sura. There is no specified
thematic or chronological order in which the chapters
are studied.

The language of the Koran is Arabic. Many believers
today still hold that translating the Koran is inadmissible.
Because not even a quarter of Muslims have Arabic as their
mother tongue, nine hundred million people must learn
Allah's eternal words by heart in a foreign language.

The Koran forms the source that feeds Islamic law.

The second most important source is from the Hadith.
The Hadith describe the life of the Prophet Mohammed
and contain a range of recommendations about how a
Muslim should conduct himself. What is written here is
known as Sunna – recommended, but not obligatory.
The Hadith are of various degrees of strength. The
'strongest' validity is lodged in Hadith that were handed
down by upright and devout Muslims and where the
sequence of authenticated transmission can be traced
back to the Prophet. If there are breaks in the path of
transmission or doubts as to the integrity of any one of
those involved in handing on the wisdom, then the
Hadith is regarded as 'weak'.

The Hadith which deal with the subject of female circumcision – known in Arabic as *khafd* – are held to be of
doubtful provenance. There are three of them. The first
deals with hygiene after sexual intercourse, the second
with the extent of circumcision. In the Hadith known as
'the tale of the circumciser' the Prophet forbids infibulation (or pharaonic circumcision) and recommends that
'if it has to be done at all' the form of circumcision should
be 'excision' (circumcision involving the inner labia and
the clitoris) – this at any rate is one interpretation of the
Hadith. The Hadith cites the Prophet as saying the circumcision should not be 'overdone' and should not lead
'to the destruction' of the genitalia. It is on this that many
muftis (Muslim legal experts) will base their view that
infibulation is forbidden, but some muftis base on it their
view that excision is recommended. Yet other Islamic
scholars think that the Hadith does not advocate a
recommendation of circumcision, but merely a limit to

the extent of circumcision, and hold that there is no mention of women having to be circumcised.

In the third Hadith female circumcision is praised as
being a noble practice to be recommended for Islamic
women. Scholars disagree about whether this Hadith
should be classed as 'weak'.

Apart from the Koran and the Hadith, a further source
of Islamic law is legal precedent (*ijtihad*), consisting of
ijma (consensus) and *qiyas* (analogy). There is no consensus on this issue; some see genital mutilation as
prescribed, some as recommended, and many other
muftis see it as a practice to be advised against. As there is
neither a specific law nor consensus, the Islamic muftis
must find an analogy and draw conclusions from existing
law. The principles of freedom from bodily harm (*hurma*)
and the ban on inflicting injuries (*la darar wa la darar*) are
important. The Egyptian Supreme Court argued in its
1997 ruling on FGM on the second of those points. Other
muftis say that FGM impinges on a woman's right to freedom from bodily harm.

Corinna gets back to me by phone later that evening.
She sounds pretty tired, and a bit bewildered. 'We have
looked through the literature you brought round,' she
says. 'We are not sure what to make of it. We will start
researching what Islamic leaders in Africa have said on
the topic. That is sure to have influenced the communities in Europe.'

A few days later we go through the results of their investigations together. There are a few positive examples, like
the Arusha conference in Tanzania in 2000, where a

declaration was made: religious leaders from a dozen countries pronounced that FGM was not a religious duty and that it encroached on the human rights of women and girls. In Chad in 2002 the imams issued an appeal in which they declared with one voice that FGM was not prescribed in the Koran. In the same year the religious leaders in Senegal likewise condemned the practice. So there is hope. But caution is needed. All these symposia and conferences were organised with the help of European development agencies.

However, in many other Islamic countries, like Mauritania, the Islamic leaders recommended the 'medicalisation' of FGM, that is, having the procedures carried out by trained health personnel in hygienic conditions. Referring to the Hadith for authority on the issue, they recommend less radical operations. This is also the tenor of religious teaching in Guinea.

The reports from the Sixteenth International Islamic Conference shocked me most. In 2004, representatives from sixty-five Islamic states gathered in Cairo, and the guidelines issued there point the way for Islam throughout the world. The slogan for the conference was 'Tolerance in Islam'. Very good, is my first reaction. They are bound to have debated women's rights. But the discussions were limited to stating that the rights of women as laid down in the Koran must be preserved, and that women must be protected from 'foreign influences' that might endanger these rights. Exactly which rights this applied to was not spelt out. They certainly did not make any pronouncement about whether protection from FGM constituted one of these rights.

This is particularly worrying in Egypt. When the Egyptian government tried for the first time in 1994 to ban FGM, a storm of indignation broke out amongst the religious leadership. Sheikh Jad Al-Haqq 'Ali Ja Al-Haqq pronounced a fatwa – an Islamic edict – to the following effect: 'Circumcision is obligatory for men and for women. If people in the villages should try to ignore this commandment, then the village Imam must fight them, dealing with them just as he would if they were to ignore the call to prayer.' This is not an Islamic speciality in Egypt. The Coptic Church had espoused FGM there for a long time. There were some Coptic priests who refused to carry out baptisms if a girl was not circumcised. However, the Coptic Church has revoked this and has spoken out now against FGM; there has been no such statement from the Islamic leaders.

'We still do not feel we know enough about this,' says Corinna. 'So we have decided we should consult an Islam expert in Europe. We have been recommended an expert in London.'

Professor David Noibi, a highly respected Islam expert, comes originally from Nigeria, where he taught Islamic law at Ibadan University before coming to Britain on a research project. The academic has been living for over ten years in London and works in the MAN mosque of the Assembly of Nigerian Muslims in Southwark, near Brixton. We take the tube to the Elephant and Castle and then go a few stops on the bus heading out of town. Rahmat Hassan, who is also from Nigeria and a central figure in the fight against FGM, accompanies us. She has set up the meeting.

Brixton is both celebrated and notorious as a part of south London where many immigrants settle. More than half the people we come across here are black. The mosque is located in a street that is wide and unadorned, home on either side to rows of small shops, among them five African and Arab hairdressers' salons. In the salons there is no room for more than one or two chairs for the clients to have their hair dressed, but each of the salons offers an additional service: an internet café with a computer, a manicure studio, or video rental service comprising just the one shelf of African tapes.

The MAN mosque is in a green, cube-shaped building that looks in need of a coat of paint. From the outside you would not realise at first glance that this is a house of prayer. We are expected, but we have to step outside first and cover our hair with borrowed headscarves.

In his simply furnished first-floor office Professor Noibi is awaiting us; there is shabby fitted carpeting, a scratched white metal table and some old pieces of furniture. The professor is engrossed in study of a large tome with Arabic script: the Koran – the volume bound in blue leather embossed with silver – a beautiful edition.

David Noibi is an impressive figure. A slim, tall man with horn-rimmed spectacles, grey hair and a well-kept beard. His floor-length white robe has embroidery on the sleeves and at the neckline and it imparts an air of a man of religion. He closes the Koran. We can speak. He tells us he is aware of the issue, because he wrote a paper at the behest of the government about sex education, and during his research for the article he looked at the issue of FGM closely.

'Why do most people who practise FGM say they do it for religious reasons?' I ask first of all.

Professor Noibi confirms what we have heard from other sources: 'The Koran does not insist on FGM. The issue is not discussed there at all. Some people still see it as an Islamic regulation because it appears in some Hadith, where there are places which make reference to circumcision. These are weak Hadith.'

'What constitutes a weak Hadith? What does that mean?'

He confirms that 'A Hadith has been handed down by word of mouth before it was ever transcribed. For this reason scholars examine the chain of transmission to see if the figures involved in handing down the pronouncements are to be relied on.'

'How is that investigated?'

'It is a process going back over hundreds of years and forms an important part of Islamic study,' replies the professor, speaking calmly. 'Scholars try to reconstruct the path by which the Hadith came down to us, and examine what is known of the lives of these people and decide whether or not the account is plausible. In the case of any doubt about the reliability of a source, the Hadith is termed a weak Hadith and does not form part of Islamic law. The Hadiths on female circumcision are held to be, as I said, weak.'

This we already knew, but what does this mean in practice? 'Is that a final judgement or do some scholars still use the Hadith as a basis for pronouncements about the way Muslims should live?' I ask.

'After the death of the Prophet four schools of Islamic

thought quickly emerged,' responds Professor Noibi. 'Disciples and adherents of the Prophet's words tried to write down everything he had said and done. Naturally, they adapted the teachings slightly to fit in with the circumstances and the customs of the regions they were living and studying in. One of these schools recommends the circumcision of women. This school of teaching is followed in large parts of Africa, and also in Asia, particularly in Malaysia and Indonesia.'

'So that means that FGM *is* advocated by certain schools of Islam?'

'Only by one school of thought, and this based on a Hadith we do not consider to be authentic. I was often attacked by my Muslim brothers here in England for saying that there was a Muslim school of thought that supported the concept of female genital mutilation. But there is no point in denying it. There are religious leaders in Africa who propagate the idea. It is better to handle the topic honestly and to say quite clearly: "The Koran does not refer to this and it is not recommended."'

'Are attempts being made within the Islamic community to eradicate the practice?' I wish to know.

'No,' says the Professor. 'In Islam there is no supreme institution that has authority to decide how the Koran is to be interpreted. This is a matter for each individual scholar, and certain directions become accepted by others.'

'What about your own view? Here in your own small congregation do you preach against FGM?'

'No, there is no one here affected by it.'

We exchange surprised glances. This is a Nigerian-mosque – and Nigeria has a high mutilation rate! Rahmat Hassan steps in: 'Yes, Professor, there *are* people here affected by it.'

The professor is amazed. He had not known this.

That is the problem – this lack of certainty, even among experts. The men do not know what FGM means for the women. As the Muslim leaders are all men, it will be a long time before they unite to speak out against FGM. But it is crucial.

At this point our talk is interrupted by the call of the muezzin, the sound ringing out loud and tinny from the speakers. The sun has gone down. It is Ramadan, the Islamic period of fasting. Devout Muslims will not have been permitted to take food or drink all day, but now, as night starts to fall, they may eat. Rahmat gets up and fetches two dates, one for her and one for the professor, for them to pop into their mouths to break the fast. The short period of time between prayers in Ramadan is now over. Professor Noibi goes over into the prayer room.

I remember the Nairobi conference against FGM that I went to in the autumn of 2004. The event was extremely moving: women from all over Africa, speaking so vehemently against FGM, in a way I had never heard before. Hassan ole Nadoo, the youth delegate of the Muslim Council in Kenya, had made a clear statement and said in his speech to the conference: For Muslims the practices of clitoridectomy and infibulation should count as *haram*, forbidden. The fight against FGM should form part of our continued struggle against superstition and oppression. In the case of the least severe form, the practice falls within the ruling of *makruhmah,* or undesirable practice, because of the risk to the future sexual relationship of the girl and her husband. As there is no hygiene or religious reason for following the custom it should be abandoned completely.' He went on to demand, 'Imams should preach against FGM with great conviction in their mosques.' All imams in the world should follow this advice. Then the problem would soon cease to exist.

7

cases must go to court

Back in Paris at last. Linda Weil-Curiel, the lawyer taking FGM cases to court in France, has already let me know that such a trial is coming up. 'You ought to be there to see what happens,' she said. So, of course I seized the opportunity and booked a flight at once.

On the day of my arrival she informs me of developments in the field. There has already been a similar case. Mr N, who stands accused together with his second wife, was born in Mali in 1947 and came to Paris in 1972. Four years later he returned to Mali, marrying his first wife there. She followed him to Paris and the couple went on to have four children, one of whom was a girl. In 1981 Mr N applied for – and was granted – French citizenship. At the same time his wife took the two-year-old girl over to Mali and arranged for mutilation to be performed, by the grandmother, according to both parents' statements. The mother declared at the time: 'If I had known it was forbidden, I would not have had it done.'

But the story does not end there. In 1992 Mr N went back to Mali and took a second wife, M, although he was now French and polygamy is illegal in France. His second wife was at this time fifteen years old. He brought her back to France and the whole family lived together in a three-room flat.

Together with his new wife, Mr N had a son and then, in 1996, a daughter, Fanta.* In 1997 Mr N took his young family home to Mali for a visit. A year later in a routine examination at one of the state-run mother and child clinics where free treatment is given it was noted by a doctor that Fanta had undergone mutilation. The mother explained to the doctor that the operation was not performed in France. 'We were staying with my husband's family and the two of us decided to spend a week in the capital, Bamako, six hundred kilometres from the village. Our little Fanta stayed behind with her grandmother; we never told her to do anything. We come back and it's too late – she has been circumcised. What could we have done?'

The doctor passed a report on the case to the authorities and that is how the first case came to court. Fanta's mother does not have French citizenship, but she could still be charged, the offence having been committed against the person of a French national, because the child was born on French soil so automatically acquires French citizenship from birth. However, the first court case did

* (not her real name)

not secure prosecution as the judge was prepared to
believe the father who said that circumcision was a matter
for the women, and nothing to do with him.

Today the case is before the courts. The second trial,
for which two days have been scheduled, takes place in
the Palais de Justice. The impressive-looking building
stands on the Ile de la Cité, the island in the middle of the
Seine in the heart of Paris. A vast ironwork gate on the
Boulevard du Palais shows a view of a courtyard and a
wide flight of stairs up to the main building. Above the
entrance stand the words: Liberté, Egalité, Fraternité –
Freedom, Equality and Brotherhood.

The courtroom is a long narrow room with panelled
walls and large gold lamps on the ceiling. I go straight
along to the visitors' section and am surprised to see there
is hardly a free seat on the wooden benches: lots of young
people are there, including a whole school class, some girl
students, a few black women, too. Altogether I count up
around seventy people there to watch. We are separated
from the actual area of the proceedings by a wooden rail.

The two accused I can only see from behind. They are
sitting directly in front of the defending counsels at grey
tables. The interpreter, a black man with glasses and wearing a dark suit, is fighting to suppress a yawn. Opposite,
representing the child, Linda, another lawyer, Fanta's
lawyer, and her officially appointed guardian, a plump
woman my own age. At the top of the room, between the
prosecution and the defence, the members of the court
judging panel: the president, an elderly man in a scarlet
robe with black sleeves, then two women judges, all in
black, then the jury, seven men and two women. The

defence, as I heard later, had already turned down some women as jurors. To the far left, on a platform with a computer in front of him, the state prosecutor. He also wears a red robe with an ermin-trimmed stole.

The doctor is the first in the witness stand. She was the one who had examined the child and discovered the abuse. Then the judge calls for M, the woman charged in the case. She gets up very slowly and goes to stand by the delicate figure of the doctor.

Now I can see her for the first time: a young, inconspicuous woman with shoulder-length hair combed straight. She is dressed completely in black and holds her jacket tight round her as if she were cold. She seems apathetic, and distant – perhaps she is afraid. She speaks slowly, quietly and indistinctly, as if it were hard to find the words she needs. 'I did not know it was forbidden,' she says. 'If I had known that, I would not have circumcised my daughter.' Just as Linda had forecast.

The judge calls female witness after witness and puts many questions and wants to know a lot of details: who said what when, who knew what at which point, who decided what, who knew nothing. And each of these African women has to answer the question: 'Are you genitally mutilated yourself?' And each of them answers, 'Yes.'

'Do you know any girls or young women from Mali who are not mutilated?' he asks the first wife of the accused man.

Her reply: 'I don't know. We don't talk about it.'

A young woman police officer presents in detail the evidence taken in witness statements at the police station. It is more or less identical with what Linda told me yesterday: Journey to Mali, one week's holiday in the capital,

Bakamo, for the parents, the grandmother took over and arranged things and apparently died in 1998.

A woman from Senegal, who grew up in Mali, then recounts in evidence the damage done to her resulting from mutilation. Initially she looks confident, but her voice becomes hoarse as she describes the agony a mutilated woman will go through in childbirth; she speaks of the day-to-day problems she experiences, and about the misconception that FGM had anything to do with religion or that it might serve any useful function. 'It is not good for anything.' The mothers who have undergone genital mutilation themselves should know how a child will suffer, she stresses, and above all she warns against leaving a girl-child with the grandmother, otherwise unsupervised. 'If I take my children to Africa, I keep them in my sight all the time.' She speaks about the role of a woman in Africa, with no rights and no authority. It is hard, she says, for these women to protect their children, 'even in Europe'. The accused woman hangs her head.

Then another female doctor gives evidence, presenting detailed descriptions of the damage caused by mutilation of the genitals. She is the last witness of the day; the case will continue tomorrow. Tomorrow the court will rule on the case.

Just as I am leaving the courtroom, Mr N crosses in front of me. He is a tall man, obviously very strong, with a powerful neck and a broad face. In his worn-out green jacket, black trousers and white sports socks he looks shabby. His brow is furrowed and there is a grim look on his face. I do not know what to think of him. Has he got any idea what was done to his daughter? Could it have been he who gave the instruction to have the operation done?

His wife walks behind him without looking at him. It is a sorry picture.

Nine-thirty a.m. and I am back in the courtroom. This time I am not sitting in the visitors' area but further forward, two rows behind Linda. From here it is easier to follow what is happening.

First a psychiatrist comes to the stand and takes the microphone. Together with a colleague, he has compiled a report about the accused couple and he discusses his findings: both normal and well-adjusted. The rest of what he says about them he embroiders with scientific expressions. It seems to me as if he is describing things, not people.

I can hardly concentrate on what he is saying; I keep having to glance over to the mother, who is sitting there motionless and with empty eyes, then over to the father, who looks even more thunderous than yesterday. He wrinkles his nose with disgust as the psychiatrist gives evidence. He does not like what he is hearing. I do not like the man.

My eyes slip back over towards the mother and it hurts to look at her. I have to think of my own mother. What if she were sitting in court, facing the same charges? Could she be held responsible for the pain and damage that was inflicted on me? Could she be found guilty, perhaps even sent to prison or given a huge fine to pay because she – yes, because she wanted to do what would be the best thing for me?

My mother wanted the best for me, I think, yet again. I know, I am a mother myself. Every mother wants the best for her child. My mother thought that by having me circumcised she was opening the way for me into the world of adulthood and she was giving me the possibility of finding a husband – for without a husband, one is nothing in our society.

Did this woman here not want just the same for her own daughter? The best?

I look at the father and again I doubt that the young wife will be able to stand up to him on anything. Did she actually have an opportunity to voice an objection to the operation? Was her opinion sought? Is she actually able to do what she considers best for her child or does the father of the child make all the decisions and present her with them? Is she a slave in his house?

The president says *Merci* and his voice brings me back to reality from the depths of my reverie. The psychiatrist has finished giving his evidence. Emanuelle Piet is called, the PMI doctor (from the mother and baby clinic) who I talked to on my last visit to Paris. She puts her view succinctly: 'I have never come across a single patient in recent years who was not aware of the law in this matter.' Linda nods; she seems satisfied.

Now it is the turn of the woman from the family planning clinic. As Linda had expected, she reports that young women come in to see her at the clinic and do not know that they have been mutilated. A boyfriend has told them they do not look normal down below.

I keep looking at the mother. What is going through her mind as she listens to this evidence? Is she becoming aware of what was done to her daughter – or indeed to herself? Does she feel guilt? Or sadness?

She lifts her head and looks at the president who is requesting her to stand. Has she learnt anything from the court case, he asks her. 'I know now that it was wrong to mutilate my child,' she mumbles.

'Why?' asks the judge.

'I have heard in these past two days many things I did not know before,' she says, haltingly. 'About physical consequences and about all the work that has been done to stop this practice. I did not know all that.'

'Would you subject your child again to the ordeal?'

'No, I would not do it again.'

'You have another little daughter. Will you have her mutilated?'

'No, I will not.'

There are tears in my eyes. I feel so sorry for her. She is petrified as she stands in front of the judge. She looks a broken woman. I believe her. I have to think of what Linda said a couple of days ago about changing the way people see. It seems to be true, but it is no consolation for me.

Why do these court cases have to happen?

M sits down again. Mr N is called to the microphone. 'What is your reaction to what your wife has just said to the court?' asks the judge.

He hesitates and then growls some answer.

'I did not hear what you said,' says the judge.

Silence, then another grunt. The president calls the interpreter over.

This is ridiculous, I say to myself. Did the psychiatrist

not just tell the court that the couple both spoke good French? Anger rises in me.

'Did you hear what your wife told the court?'

He did not. He was obviously not listening. A murmur goes through the courtroom. Finally, the judge manages to extract a sentence from him: 'Mutilation is not good.' But his voice lacks conviction.

I am furious. He seems to have taken no notice of the whole proceedings! Does he not care what happened to his wives, what happened to his daughters? He has sat through the whole court case without taking anything in, without understanding anything. He is never going to change, I think. Then I remember why it is crucial to bring these cases before the courts. There are people who will never learn. And how are their children to be protected?

Linda gets up and tells the court about the work she does and the fight against FGM and about what has been done to eradicate the practice in some African states. She shows the jury posters that have been on display in France and in African countries. Then she turns to the parents with a poem. Neither of them shows any emotion. But I am convinced that M is listening attentively.

The spectators in the courtroom are becoming restless. Now we have the final pleas – the climax of the case. First it is the turn of the young lawyer who has been sitting next to Linda all the time we have been here. 'I stand here as a lawyer, as a woman and as a citizen,' she says, starting her speech. 'As a lawyer, defending the rights of a child, as a woman who can feel sympathy, and as a citizen, who cannot stand by and do nothing when the rights of others are violated.'

'The parents,' she says, 'are guilty of having committed an offence.' They had failed in their duty to protect their child from harm, and had broken French law. 'The mutilation is definite, dramatic and irreparable.'

She questions the plausibility of the parents' statement that they had not known of the illegality of their action. 'It was probably coincidental that they travelled to Mali with one child, leaving seven at home, coincidental that they left the child unsupervised with the grandmother, and it was purely coincidental that they were confronted with the done deed on their return to the village.'

Mr N's first wife had said she knew the practice was illegal in France, the lawyer reminds the court. 'She knew that when they left for Africa. The mother knew what she was doing; she knew that it wasn't permitted. The information is on the grapevine in African circles. All the women know.'

Neither of the accused reacts.

'But,' she continues, 'there is a difference between the two parents. The accused mother is thirty years younger than her husband. She is his second wife. She was fifteen, and when she arrived in France the first wife was there. We can imagine the difficulties she will have had, the humiliation and the sword of Damocles hanging over her: in the case of a separation from her husband she loses the right to be in France. She is totally subordinate to the will of a husband who could have been her father. But she could have protected her child; she could have been more vigilant. She too is responsible for what happened.

'The father – a different case. Eating in the African way, dressing in the African way and then talking of first

and second wives, as if that were normal. This shows that
he is living according to African behaviour patterns. He
has told us he knew that genital mutilation is banned in
France. The family is living under his patriarchy. It was he
who made the decision about having the procedure done.
I remind the court: he is a French citizen! A taxi driver. A
taxi driver who speaks no French? He paid for everything.
He did not take his sons to Africa to have them
circumcised.'

Now it is the turn of the counsel representing the
interests of the child. He entirely endorses everything
said by his colleague. However, in his conclusion he tells
the court, 'In my view the best solution would be that the
court should not impose payment of a large sum in damages as this would cause great hardship to the family.'

I glance at Linda. She is fuming.

Finally, the state prosecutor stands up to address the
court. He presents background information, speaking of
the clashing values of two conflicting cultures: French
and African. A comparison between Western culture, pri-
oritising the rights of the individual and defence of a
person's physical integrity – and African culture with its
emphasis on traditions and the customs respected in a
family. 'The role of the individual there is not the same as
it is in our society.'

Then the central question: 'How great is the responsibility of the parents in this case?' The prosecution gives
detailed information about the background, then says,
'They have made themselves accomplices, conniving in
this act of mutilation, by taking their daughter to an
environment where it would be possible.'

'Did they know that the practice was illegal?' the prosecutor asks.

'Yes, I am sure that they did know. In the case of the father I am totally convinced that he knew. And in the case of the child's mother? I am sceptical about her statement that she had not been aware it was against the law.'

Then he states his petition as to the penalty. 'The ban must be upheld. Fanta is a French national, to be protected by French law. It is the right of every person to have the freedom to decide what is to happen to his or her own body. The use of force must be punished. A dimension of the girl's physical senses has been amputated, namely the ability to experience sexual desire. This is not acceptable. For this reason I propose imprisonment.'

He asks for a five-year sentence for Mr N. The defendant should further lose his civil rights such as the right to vote or to stand for election. The state prosecutor then takes his seat again.

The court is silent. The prosecution has said everything there was to be said. I am relieved. The mother has been treated fairly. In my eyes she is more a victim than a criminal. Unlike her husband. The evidence is overwhelming. This is why I am so interested to hear what his defence counsel will have to say.

'No one is claiming that it is a good tradition,' he begins. 'But it is the defendant's mother who actually committed the offence.'

Aha, I think. So that is his strategy. He wants to sow the seeds of doubt. Doubt goes in favour of the defendant.

The defence lawyer speaks of the great significance

accorded to traditional customs and urges the court to
take into account the 'culture, the roots' of the defendant. He mentions that in Mali people believe in witches
and magic. 'How could conflict have been avoided
between French law and African custom?'

Then defence counsel for the wife. She is also young,
twenty-eight, as she is about to tell us. She speaks of simi-
larities between herself and the woman on trial: they are
the same age; both have families, both have a daughter.
And then of the differences between them: the woman
facing charges has had no schooling, cannot read, was
forced at the age of fifteen to marry a man much older
than herself and to move to France, to the home and the
animosity of the man's first wife. She had no contact with
the outside world, nobody she could turn to. 'How could
she have stood up to her family, stood up to this man?'

The woman, however, had, in the course of the trial,
'shown development. She has told the court she will not
inflict circumcision on her youngest daughter.' Her personal circumstances had also recently undergone a
change and she was now working as a cleaner, earning
money, and was coming into contact with other people, a
positive step.

That is the last plea. Now it is up to the jury to consider
their verdict. The session is over and the court withdraws.
It is evening now and the courtroom has grown cold. The
few members of the public who have stayed to the end of
the proceedings now get up to leave. The two defendants
remain seated, in silence, deep in thought. How long the
verdict will take we do not know, but the judge will only
accept a unanimous decision.

It takes more than five hours. The court's decision follows the prosecution's recommendation of a suspended
sentence of five years and loss of civil rights for the husband, and a one-year suspended sentence for the
mother.

Linda is satisfied by the judge's decision. For her work
she is paid one symbolic euro, while the parents will have
to pay costs of one thousand euros to CAMS. 'The court
has taken the defence's arguments into consideration but
has still imposed a penalty,' she says. 'It is a fair judgment.'

'And if the father puts a foot wrong in the next five
years, he goes straight to prison.'

I am exhausted. I am feeling the effects of the strain of
the past months. Back in my hotel room I collapse on to
the bed. Hundreds of thoughts are still rushing round
my head. All the pain I have heard about, the desolate situation in the African ghettos, but also the courage and
determination of the victims I have come across.

Yes, I tell myself. It is worth fighting for all these girls
and women. From them I get the strength I need to carry
on. This journey is far from over.

I drift off to sleep, jolted awake some time later. I had
nearly forgotten that I am meeting Kadi today. She was
the first FGM victim that I met via the web. I had been
immediately caught up by her story. She has been on my
mind so often in the intervening months and today we
are to meet face to face.

We have arranged to meet in the hotel bar. Kadi is not
alone – a friend is coming along with her. I recognise the

two of them at once as they walk into the lobby: Kadi is a small-framed woman of twenty, with shining eyes and long hair combed straight. Her friend Sata (not her real name) is somewhat younger and taller, dressed in dark brown and black. She has dark skin and shoulder-length curly hair worn in a plait. She is from Senegal.

We sit in a corner, away from the businessmen at the bar marking the end of their working day with a beer or a whisky. Kadi and Sata settle down in the big leather chairs, exchange glances and giggle. 'Did you find the hotel OK?' I ask them.

'Yes, we found it straightaway,' Kadi replies and then asks me, 'How long have you been here?'

'I got here on Saturday. I've been at the law courts yesterday and today, following a case.' While I tell them about it the mood gets easier and more relaxed. I can see they are both interested and it breaks the ice. They do not give the impression they have only come to meet me and have a chat – they want to discuss the issue that concerns them: genital mutilation.

'You may not believe it, but we've only just started talking to each other about our own excisions because we were coming here to see you today. Honestly – we had never spoken of it before. And we've been friends for ages. It's done us both such good to talk about it together,' says Kadi, and Sata nods in agreement.

They tell me they have known each other since they were small because their families were neighbours. Kadi is training to be a social worker and Sata has just finished school and is waiting to start a business studies course.

Kadi tells us about her cousin who has four daughters,

two of them in France and two back in Mali. The two eldest are already mutilated, but the two young ones, at one and a half and then a new baby, are not. Her cousin is in favour of genital mutilation, Kadi says, because she is convinced that if the clitoris is intact then a woman can't give birth naturally, but only by Caesarean section. 'I've tried to tell her that FGM is a bad thing and I've told her about the health problems that can result. But only when I told her "It's like a society deciding it is better for children to live with just one eye, so they cut the second one out" – that made her stop and think.'

'You see,' I said, 'how important it is to educate people. People must be told what FGM really is. Information is crucial in the fight against this crime. As long as there are ideas like your cousin's floating about, we will go on seeing FGM practised.'

Then I remember the court case and the father with his total lack of insight into what he had done, so I continue: 'But it is not enough.' I pick up the story of how the trial went, the attitude of the father and things he had said. Then I asked the girls if FGM was ever spoken of at home.

'We never mention it. I would love to know what my brothers think about the subject. And I could never speak to my father about it.'

The situation is similar in Sata's family. 'We don't talk about it either. You can't.'

Especially not with the men, they both agree. 'There are lots of men who would never marry a woman who hasn't been circumcised. They say she is unclean,' adds Sata.

'I've got an eighteen-year-old sister who hasn't been circumcised,' Kadi tells me. 'This summer she went to Mali for the first time. I've got another older married sister there – she's thirty-five and grew up in Mali. She told the eighteen-year-old she won't find a husband because she has male genitals. She even told her, "Don't worry – we'll have you done, and then you will get a husband."'

We fall silent for a moment. 'Do you still remember?' I ask, and everyone knows what I mean. Both of them nod their heads.

Sata begins talking first. She was mutilated when she was eight. In Africa. At the age of fourteen she saw a TV documentary about circumcision and all the memories she had suppressed so well all those years came flooding back. 'I was not prepared for it at all. I don't remember any more how I got there or what the place was like. But what happened – yes, I certainly remember that. Not the pain, but the scene. They took hold of me by the arms and legs. I think I was crying and screaming so much that I wasn't really so aware of the pain. It was terrible – I lost masses of blood.'

It had been carried out very badly. 'When I went back to Senegal in 1999 they even asked me if I wanted it re-done, because such a bad job had been made of it the first time. But even my parents said no, then.'

'Do you both remember who it was performed the operation?' I ask.

'It was an old woman with a finger missing,' says Kadi.

'How long were you in Senegal?'

'At least four months,' Sata estimates.

'Yes, me too,' says Kadi.

'My younger sister stayed even longer, a year or more,' recalls Sata.

'Is it hard for you to talk about it?' I ask them.

'No, it feels good!' replies Kadi, and grins at me. 'If you keep it all to yourself it makes you feel bad.'

'Same here,' agrees Sata. 'There was a time my head seemed to be bursting; I had so many questions . . . Then I talked about it to a friend from Algeria, who hadn't been circumcised. She couldn't understand it at all and changed the subject at once. I found that hurtful.'

'But why did you two not talk about it together?'

'Well, you know, these are things you try to forget,' says Kadi. 'In my class at school they knew that girls get mutilated in Mali. They asked me if it had happened to me. I couldn't tell them, so I said no. I was afraid I would be treated differently if I told the truth.'

'When did you become aware that FGM is a bad thing?'

'When I was fourteen,' says Sata. 'I started having nightmares.'

'What kind of mutilation were you subjected to?'

'For me they only took away the clitoris,' answers Sata.

'My family left it up to the circumciser,' Kadi elaborates, 'and she cut off the clitoris and the inner labia.'

I am surprised how easily the two girls are able to talk about it, smiling at me all the time. I am proud of them both.

We sit back in our leather armchairs and relax. The waiter comes over.

'Would you like to order anything else to drink?' Kadi and Sata shake their heads.

'Can we have the bill, then, please?' I say to him, and turn to the girls. 'Are you hungry, maybe?'

They look at each other and laugh.

'That sounds like very hungry. Let's go and eat!'

epilogue

I have a dream

For over six months I have put the rest of my life on hold and given priority to a single task. This has brought me probably the biggest challenge I have met so far.

Today I know that there is a time-bomb ticking away in Europe. The sound it makes is rhythmical and clear: tick tock, tick tock, tick tock. But no one is listening. Because no one can stand to hear the truth.

Today I know that genital mutilation is not just a problem confined to Africa, but one which affects the whole world.

Today I know that in Germany alone the number of women affected by genital mutilation will double in ten years.

Today I know that FGM is a practice found in every European land. Families that can afford it have their daughters mutilated in the clinics of the rich or go to a private doctor. Families who have less money will get the cruel job done in the back streets somewhere, or else send their girls back to Africa, for the grandmother to sort out.

Today I know that awareness of the issue of genital mutilation is shockingly inadequate. Even among health professionals whose job brings them into contact with it. There is a marked lack of training in the subject for doctors, nursing staff, and social workers, and this leads to many incidents of them reacting inappropriately and tactlessly when dealing with victims of FGM.

Today I know that the victims need help – from us all. I am prepared to give my help. My journey is over but my mission is only just beginning. I pledge my strength and energy to the cause of eradicating genital mutilation throughout the world and particularly in Europe.

I have a dream and this time I am wide awake. In my dream I see a film about genital mutilation. I see the brutal ceremony of mutilation and all the blood, I can hear the screams. I see a black family: father, mother, son, daughter. When the film is over, the children stare at their parents, horrified. 'You don't have to be afraid,' says the father. 'That doesn't happen anymore – that's what it used to be like. In the old days, girls were cut and mutilated in that way when they were very young. Thank God no one does it any more.'

'But why did they do that?' the daughter wants to know.

'No idea,' the father says, shaking his head thoughtfully. 'I've got no idea at all.'

The Waris Dirie Manifesto

'You will not see the whole picture unless you step out of the frame,' writes Salman Rushdie in *The Ground Beneath her Feet*.

It is time to step out of the frame. I have a long road ahead of me. I have very clear ideas of what I want to achieve in my fight against Genital Mutilation in Europe.

Here are my fifteen goals:

I want:

- everyone in Europe to recognise genital mutilation as a problem common to all countries and one we can no longer shut our eyes to;
- every religious community to take a clear stand against the practice of genital mutilation;
- every FGM victim needing help to get the help she needs;
- all European governments to issue regulations to protect girls from genital mutilation – in Europe and abroad;
- all European governments to pass legislation enabling perpetrators and their accomplices to be brought to justice;
- it to be mandatory for every incident that comes to light of mutilation of a minor to be reported for prosecution;
- all European countries to regard genital mutilation as equal to political persecution and as grounds for asylum;
- everyone to be enlightened about the status of genital mutilation: not culture, but torture;

- all genital mutilation victims at last to be treated with sensitivity and respect;
- all health workers to become well informed about FGM and to know how to help victims;
- all victims, where it is their wish, to have free access to surgery to counteract the damage and to receive psychological counselling;
- genital mutilation to be a subject that people can and will openly discuss;
- all the groups working to combat FGM to come together and agree on their policy and strategies;
- all organisations working to combat FGM to have sufficient funding to be able to function efficiently;
- everyone in Europe to put into action my dream of an end to genital mutilation.

If this book can start the ball rolling, I will be the happiest person in the world.

appendix I

1. What is female genital mutilation (FGM)?
According to the definition given by the World Health
Organisation, female genital mutilation is the designated
term for any procedures under which female genitalia
are wholly or partly removed or damaged, whether for
cultural reasons or for any reasons other than medical.

The term FGM using the English initial letters was
introduced because the terminology 'female circumcision' was considered by many victims to trivialise the issue,
given that the most common forms of male circumcision
are considerably less traumatic. 'Female genital cutting' is
a term also employed, with the aim of avoiding overtones
of the word 'mutilation', distasteful to some victims.
Another term in use, particularly in France, is 'female
sexual mutilation', the thinking being that it refers not

only to physical damage but also to the damage to a woman's sexual nature and responses.

The World Health Organisation (WHO) has divided FGM into four classes:
Type I: Cutting out the hood of the clitoris and the clitoris itself wholly or in part.
Type II: Cutting out the clitoris hood, the clitoris and the labia minora, or parts of these.
Eighty percent of women victims have undergone either Type I or Type II.
Type III: Cutting out parts or the whole of the genitalia, with subsequent stitching together of the opening to leave a tiny hole (Infibulation). In this procedure, usually the inner labia are completely removed and the outer labia are sewn together so that scar tissue covers the entrance to the vagina. Girls who undergo this are often forced to lie for weeks with their legs bound together. To avoid the orifice closing completely, a foreign body, such as a matchstick or a straw, is introduced, The resulting hole serves as an exit for urine and menstrual blood, which will only be able to leave the body in small drops. This procedure, considered the severest form of FGM, is suffered by about fifteen percent of victims.
Type IV: Incision, perforation, nicking, stretching, scarring of the genitalia with burns to the clitoris or labia, scraping the flesh away on the vaginal opening, introducing corrosive substances or herbs with the aim of tightening the vagina, and any other process entailing injury to or cutting of the female genitalia.

2. What are the consequences of FGM?

FGM causes grave psychological and physical damage to the victim. It is the purpose of the mutilation procedure to impair the sexuality of the woman. Over and above this, FGM can result in serious health problems for the woman. Amnesty International has listed the most common harmful effects:

During and immediately following mutilation:

Heavy blood loss, shock, injuries to the urethra, bladder, anal sphincter, Bartholin glands, and vulva; tetanus, serious pain, infection of the wound, infection of the urinary tract, blood poisoning, urine retention, fever, death following as a result of shock or tetanus or other infections; fractures to thigh or collar bone as a consequence of forcible restraint: delayed healing due to secondary infection, anaemia and malnourishment. With the process of infibulation the death rate is thirty percent.

Following healing of the wound, and in adult life:

Infections of the bladder and the inner genital region, pain on intercourse, vulvovaginal abscesses and cysts, cheloid formation (fibrous scar tissue over a wound), neurinoma (benign tumour forming on a severed nerve – for example the nerves of the clitoris – which can lead to extreme sensitivity of the area), narrowing of the vagina, retention of blood or pus in the vagina, infertility, formation of fistules, chronic infections of the urinary tract, incontinence, retention of urine, hypersensitivity of genital area, anal fissures, faecal incontinence.

At childbirth:

Increased risk of transmission of sexually transmitted diseases and HIV infections, tears to the tissue, increased blood loss, wounds breaking open, increased length of delivery time, extreme stress to the pelvic floor, increased stress to the foetus.

Psychological problems:
Trauma, feeling of incompleteness, fear, depression, chronic irritability, frigidity, relationship conflicts, psychosis.

3. Why is FGM performed?

In the communities that practise FGM it is a deeply rooted tradition originally signifying a rite of passage into adulthood, and thus a ritual involving a celebration. This ritual background has now disappeared in many regions, but in spite of that the practice of FGM is retained. In these cultures it is seen as a pre-requisite for marriage, with unmutilated women regarded as unclean and as whores, and excluded from society. The following reasons are cited for performing FGM: to ensure the chastity of the woman, to ensure the preservation of virginity until marriage, or for hygiene, aesthetic or health reasons. In some countries it is believed that an uncircumcised woman will not be able to give birth or that contact with the clitoris will be fatal for the baby.

4. Who performs FGM?

Traditionally, the rite is performed by female circumcisers. These women enjoy high social status, but for the most part they have no medical training and they work with inadequate instruments such as razor blades or fragments of glass. In urban areas in Africa a growing trend towards 'medicalisation' has been observed: FGM is increasingly carried out in hospitals. In Europe FGM is either carried out by circumcisers or by doctors, usually from the same countries of origin as the families and, evidently, increasing numbers of women apply to cosmetic surgery clinics.

5. Medical care

Victims of FGM often need intensive medical care from specialists. Those working in health provision in Europe are often not prepared for meeting the needs of women who have been genitally mutilated. In several countries, however, the subject now forms part of the course for medical students training as doctors – for example, in Austria and Germany – and for midwives (in Austria).

Infibulations can be re-opened: a process known as de-infibulation. This involves cutting through the scar tissue to expose the genital region lying beneath it. The operation itself is not complicated, but some degree of psychological counselling is imperative. Only one doctor in Europe offers an operation entailing the re-building of the clitoris: Dr Pierre Foldès, in St-Germain-en-Laye, just outside Paris. Contact addresses are to be found in the address section.

The French National Academy for Medicine issued a declaration in 2004 that may serve as a catalogue of good practice for other countries:

1. Overall, institute education campaigns to:
• inform people of the extent and the characteristics of mutilations encountered in Europe;

- encourage studies and investigative research in the relevant countries;
- introduce the topic of FGM and its effects into the training programmes for health workers.

2. Improve information about FGM circulated in the public sector:
- particularly in the areas of health, education, the media, justice and social work;
- publicise penalties and damages imposed by court rulings;
- raise awareness of how the problem of FGM is being tackled in the countries of origin;
- involve celebrities with influence in the communities;
- raise public awareness of the groups already working on the issue such as non-governmental organisations, charities and anti-FGM pressure groups.

3. Incorporate the newly won knowledge of the issue into treatment and diagnosis in the medical sector thus:
- no health worker may participate in any form of genital mutilation surgery as per the directive from the World Health Organisation;
- if a patient reports gynaecological or urinary problems, the doctor should consider the possibility that genital mutilation may have been carried out – NB country of origin;
- where a case of genital mutilation is diagnosed, the woman should be given information about her condition; the health worker should investigate what limitations the condition places on the victim and

should discuss the viability of an operation to re-open a sewn genital orifice where appropriate;
- in the case of pregnancy and childbirth the woman should be reminded that circumcision is illegal for the baby if it should be a girl;
- never omit examination of the genital area;
- any discovered case of female genital mutilation performed on a minor *must* be reported to the relevant authorities.

4. Enable repair surgery to be developed:
- continue to research techniques of repair and reconstructive surgery and train more doctors in their use;
- enable the costs for repair operations to be borne out of the public purse and health insurance schemes.

5. Demand effective prevention policy from the authorities:
- remind the authorities to inform immigrants at the port of entry into Europe – and on exit from Europe – of the legal implications of having FGM operations performed;
- harmonise preventative measures and efforts Europe-wide.

appendix II

The situation is different now from a few years ago when there was still debate about whether or not FGM should be an offence punishable by law. Six European countries now have specific legislation covering FGM; in the other countries the offence is covered by legislation on the infliction of actual bodily harm. Rulings in individual countries as follows:

Belgium: At the end of 2000, Article 409 was added to the Belgian Penal Code, unambiguously declaring the practice of genital mutilation to be punishable by law. The European Parliament has made it clear that further action is still required; in 2003 Belgium was expressly instructed to strengthen the measures in force designed to protect girls at risk.

Denmark: No specific ruling; FGM comes under §245 of the Penal Code (bodily harm).

Germany: FGM is punishable under legislation covering offences against the person and the right to physical integrity (§223ff StGB – the Penal Code). Doctors performing the procedure stand to lose their licences to practise for between one and five years. According to the lawyer Regina Kalthegener, there have been indications since 1995 that FGM is also being practised in Germany. She was told by a credible source in Italy that a genital mutilation procedure was being arranged in a town in North Germany – however, the Public Prosecutor's office showed little interest in pursuing the matter because of concern that police involvement in the investigation might be seen as racist. A similar attitude was displayed on a different occasion in Karlsruhe. In Berlin in 1999 a gynaecologist was under observation, having been filmed in secret as he negotiated a price of €610 in today's money for conducting an FGM operation. The case was dropped for lack of sufficient evidence to secure a conviction. Due to data loss the doctor was unable to produce details of patients.

Finland: No specific legislation. The offence is covered by Penal Code clauses dealing with bodily harm. In 1992 the Ministry for Health and Social Affairs circulated notification to all hospitals that FGM was illegal.

France: Under Articles 222–9 and 222–10 of the Penal Code, FGM is illegal and since 1979 has been a punishable offence that is actively pursued through the courts. Here France differs from other European countries. Examples of prosecutions: There was great interest and

commotion caused in 1991 by a number of cases in which
a female circumciser and the parents of seventeen girls
were taken to court. The woman was given four years'
imprisonment and the parents one-year suspended sentences. In 1993, for the first time a mother was given a
one-year prison sentence and a further four years' probation. The prosecution of a circumciser in 1999 resulted in
eight years' imprisonment; in this case the mother of the
mutilated girl was sent to jail for two years with a further
three-year suspended sentence.

Greece: No specific legislation for the offence.

United Kingdom: FGM is punishable under a specific law,
the Prohibition of Female Circumcision Act of 1985. In
2003 the name was altered to Prohibition of Female
Genital Mutilation Act and the scope extended to include
acts of mutilation performed abroad. The new law came
into force in March 2004. So far there have been no prosecutions in British courts.

The Republic of Ireland: No specific legislation.

Italy: No special law; the offence is covered by legislation
on bodily harm.

Luxemburg: No specific article in the Penal Code; covered
by clause governing bodily harm.

Netherlands: No specific legislation. FGM is covered by legislation on bodily harm and is punishable under Articles
300 to 309 of the Penal Code. There was a great deal of
controversy when the Dutch Ministry of Health tabled a
proposal in 1992 that a 'non-mutilating form' of FGM be
legalised – the procedure concerned entailing a small
incision in the clitoris. The intention was that FGM could
be carried out under hygienic conditions and that many

Somali immigrants would give up the practice of infibulation. There was strong feeling on the issue and protests
were lodged at home and abroad. After a year's delibera-
tion, the government took a clear stand against any form
of mutilation.

Norway: FGM itself and aiding and abetting FGM are
specifically prohibited in legislation dating from 1995.
Norwegian citizens who commit the offence abroad are
equally liable to prosecution. It had been possible to
bring charges before that time under existing laws, but
the formulation of new legislation was intended to make
a point and to ensure increased public awareness.

Austria: Since 2001 any instance of FGM likely to cause
lasting impairment of sexual sensation has been explicitly
prohibited under §90 of the Austrian Penal Code. It is not
possible for permission to be given by the patient herself
for the operation to be carried out.

Portugal: No special legislation; the laws governing bodily
harm will apply (Article 143 of the Penal Code).

Sweden: The Swedish government prohibited FGM in
1992, under the special 'Law prohibiting female circumcision'. In 1998/99 the penalties were increased. FGM
performed on Swedish nationals outside the country is
proscribed in just the same way. No prosecutions have yet
taken place.

Switzerland: No special law. The offence is covered by
existing legislation on assault (Articles 122 and 123 of
the Penal Code), irrespective of whether the operation
is conducted for cultural reasons or on therapeutic
grounds.

Spain: No special legislation. The charge of assault as

under Section IV, Article 421, §2 can be applied. In 2003 the European parliament demanded better protection for girls at risk.

appendix III

WHO WILL HELP?

Austria
African Women's Organisation in Vienna
Afrikanische Frauenorganisation in Wien
• advice centre (funded by the city of Vienna)
• preventative work, surveys commissioned for the EU
Türkenstr. 3
A-1090 WIEN
Tel.: +43-1-310 51 45

Orient Express
• advice centre for immigrant women
• advice, care, accompaniment to appointments etc.
• advice given in German, Turkish, Arabic and English
• advice is confidential and free of charge
Hillerstr. 6/3-5

A-1020 Wien
Tel.: +43-1-728 97 25
www.orientexpress-wien.com
office@orientexpress-wien.com

Amnesty for women – working group for Austria
AG Frauen amnesty international Österreich
• arranges advice and help with asylum applications
Moeringgasse 10/1
A-1150 Wien
Tel.: +43-1-780 08
www.amnesty.at/ag-frauen
ag-frauen@amnesty.a

Österreichische Plattform gegen Genitalverstümmelung
Umbrella organisation for anti-FGM groups and individuals.
Contact:
National assembly member Petra Bayr
Schenkenstr.8
A-1010 Wien
Tel.: +43-1-401 10-36 85
www.stopfgm.net
petra.bayr@parlament.gv.at

Germany
Terre des Femmes
Women's organisation with an anti-FGM campaign.
• Publicity campaigns
• Teaching materials for schools and health workers
• Information for immigrant women

PO Box 2565
D-72015 Tübingen
Tel.: +49-7071-797 30
Fax: +49-7071-7973 22
www.frauenrechte.de

FORWARD Germany
Foundation for Women's health, research and development.
• Active in UK and in Nigeria since 1985
• In Germany since 1998
• Education work for African women
• Girls' project and family centre
Martin-Luther-Str.35
D-60389 Frankfurt am Main
www.forward-germany.de

INTACT e.V.
International Action against circumcision of women and girls.
Organisation chaired by Christa Müller
• Education work concentrated in Benin, but also in Germany
Johannisstr.4
D-66111 Saarbrücken
Tel.: +49-681-324 00
Fax: +49-681-938 80 02
www.intact-ev.de
info@intact-ev.de

stop mutilation e.V. – Düsseldorf
Group for Somali women.
• Education campaigns in Germany and Somalia
• Information for various professions
J. Cumar
Gustorferstr. 12
D-40549 Düsseldorf
Tel.: +49-211-506 57 45
www.stop-mutilation.org
j.cumar@stop-mutilation.org

DAFI Deutsch-Afrikanische-Frauen-Initiative
DAFI advises women from Africa and offers information
for professional groups.
Prinzenallee 81
D-13357 Berlin
Tel.: +49-30-294 02 59
dafi_berlin@yahoo.de

DAFNEP (Deutsch-Afrikanisches Frauen-Netzwerk-Projekt)
• Medical advice and education campaigns for African
  women in Berlin
Mariatu Rohde
Wildpfad 7
D-14193 Berlin
Tel.: +43-30-825 57 65
and +49-30-89 72 99 70
MariatuRohde@web.de
and mariatur@web.de

Familienplanungszentrum Balance e.V
- Family planning
- Women affected by the issue are treated by German doctors who are competent and caring
- Psychological-social care and/or medical treatment
- Advice – sessions by appointment

Mauritius-Kirch-Str.3
D-10365 Berlin
Tel.: +49-30-553 67 92
www.fpz-berlin.de
balance@fpz-berlin.de

Society for the Rights of African Women
G.R.A.F.e.V (Gesellschaft für die Rechte Afrikanischer Frauen)
- African women, including a female doctor from Cameroon, advise African women on FGM, and HIV/AIDS and offer support in times of difficulty.

Kaiserdamm 24
D-14057 Berlin
Tel.: +49-30-30 11 39 40
Or +49-30-88 68 7700
www.graf-berlin.de
graf_brd@yahoo.de

Public Health Department, Frankfurt
Stadtgesundheitsamt Frankfurt
- Advice centre for African women
- A Kenyan health worker employed by the department advises men and women from Africa on general health questions, HIV/AIDS and FGM.

Braubachstr. 18-22
Zimmer 303
D-60311 Frankfurt am Main
Tel.: +49-69-21 24 52 41

AGISRA e.V. – Köln (Arbeitsgemeinschaft gegen internationale sexuelle und rassistische Ausbeutung)
A group campaigning against international sexist and racist exploitation.
• Advice and support for immigrants, including on the topic of FGM
Steinbergerstr.40
D-50733 Köln
Tel.: +49-221-12 40 19
Or +49-2221-139 03 92
www.agisrakoeln.de
agisra@e-migrantinnen.de

France
GAMS Groupe Femmes pour l'Abolition des Mutilations Sexuelles
French section of the Interafrican Committee against Harmful Traditions.
• Public awareness campaigns
• Advice
66, rue des Grands-Champs
F-75020 Paris
Tel.: +33-1-43 48 10 87
www.perso.wanadoo.fr/associationgams/

CAMS – Commission pour l'Abolition des Mutilations Sexuelles
- Legal representation in court for minors, filing parallel suits
- Raising public awareness

President: Linda Weil-Curiel
6, Place St.Germain-des-Près
F-750006 Paris
Tel.: +33-1-45 49 04 00
www.cams-fgm.org
linda.weil.curiel@cams-fgm.org

Equilibres et populations
Development organisation with a focus on FGM.
205, Boulevard St Germain
F-75007 Paris
Tel.: +33-1-53 63 80 40
Fax: +33-1-53 63 80 50
info@equipop.org
www.equipop.org

Institut Théramex
Institute for women's health.
- Research, conferences and training
- FGM is a focus

38-40 Avenue de New York
F-75016 Paris
Tel.: +33-1-53 67 63 32
www.institut-theramex.com

United Kingdom
Amnesty International Secretariat
Human Rights organisation working on FGM since 1995
worldwide.
1, Easton Street
London WC1X 8DJ
Tel.: +44-20-74 13 55 00
Fax: +44-20-79 56 11 57
www.amnesty.org
office@amnesty.org

FORWARD
• Political campaigning, awareness-raising
• Advice for women affected by GM
Unit 4, 765-767 Harrow Road
London NW10 5NY
Tel.: +44-208-960 4000
www.forwarduk.org.uk
forward@forwarduk.org.uk

RAINBO
Research, Action and Information Network for the Bodily
Integrity of Women.
• Works to combat FGM by supporting self-esteem of
  African women
Suite 5A Queens Studios
121 Salisbury Road
London NW6 6RG
Tel.: +44-207 625 3400
www.rainbo.org
info@rainbo.org

Black Women's Health and Family Organisation
- Works with African women, particularly towards prevention of FGM
- Advice on social issues

1st Floor, 82 Russia Lane
London E2 9LU
Tel.: +44-208 980 3503

Women Living under Muslim Law
International solidarity network for women whose lives are governed or affected by laws which are actually or purportedly derived from Islam.
International Coordination Office
PO Box 28445
London N10 5NZ
www.wluml.org
wluml@wluml.org

Clinics:
The African Well Woman Clinic
Comfort Momoh,
Office 3, 6th Floor, North Wing
St. Thomas Hospital
London SE1 7EH
Tel.: +44-207-960 5595

Elizabeth Garrett Anderson African Women's Clinic/
Women and Health
Sarah Creighton
Contact: Maligaye Bikoo, Clinical Nurse Specialist
Huntley Street

London WC1E 6DH
Tel.: +44-2077 387 9300
maligaye.bikoo@uclh.nhs.uk

Harry Gordon Antenatal Clinic
Central Middlesex Hospital
Acton Lane, Park Royal
London NW10 7NS
Tel.:+44-208 965 5733

Susan Dolman Antenatal Clinic
Northwick Park & St Marks Hospitals
Watford Road
Harrow
Middlesex HA1 3UJ
Tel.: +44-208 869 2880

Lydia Moore Multi-Cultural Antenatal Clinic
Liverpool Women's Hospital
Crown Street
Liverpool L8 755

How to support Waris Dirie in her work
If you feel you would like to help Waris Dirie in her campaign against female genital mutilation you can do so by sending a donation to Germany as follows:

>Waris Dirie Foundation
>Dresdner Private Banking
>Account number: 405 564 000
>Bank sort code (BLZ): 500 803 00

Or to Austria/Switzerland:

>Waris Dirie Foundation
>Bank Austria Creditanstalt
>Account number: 50333 903 555
>Bank sort code (BLZ): 12000
>IBAN:AT 30 1200 0503 33903555
>BIC: BKAUATWW

You can find more information about the work of the Waris Dirie Foundation and details of current campaigns at www.desertflowerfoundation.org.

You can reach Waris Dirie by email at waris@utanet.at

I am Brother of Belu Pereira she is Balarón
from 1d B1 I'm calling to let you kho
that she will be absent today Because
she doesn't feel well Thank you.